JESUS IN FOCUS
A LIFE IN ITS SETTING

Gerard S. Sloyan

JESUS IN FOCUS

A LIFE IN ITS SETTING

TWENTY-THIRD PUBLICATIONS
Mystic, Connecticut

Cover photo by James Nisbet
Woodcut by Robert McGovern
Edited by John G. van Bemmel and Carol Clark
Designed by John G. van Bemmel

ISBN 0-89622-194-6
Library of Congress Catalog Card Number 83-70619

Contents

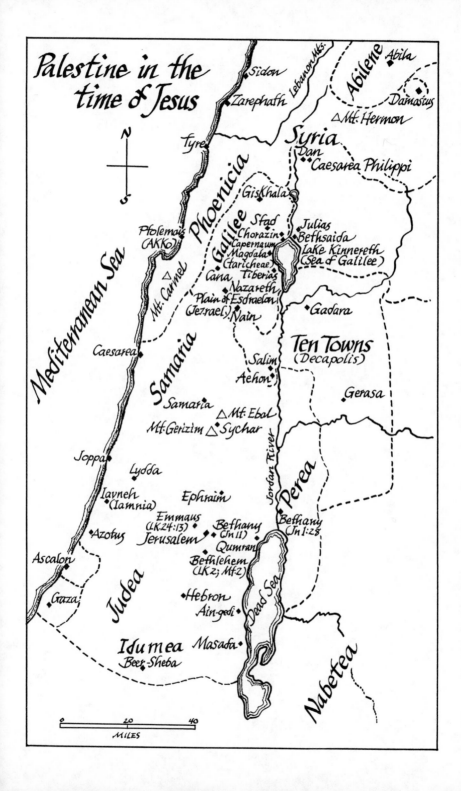

Palestine in the time of Jesus

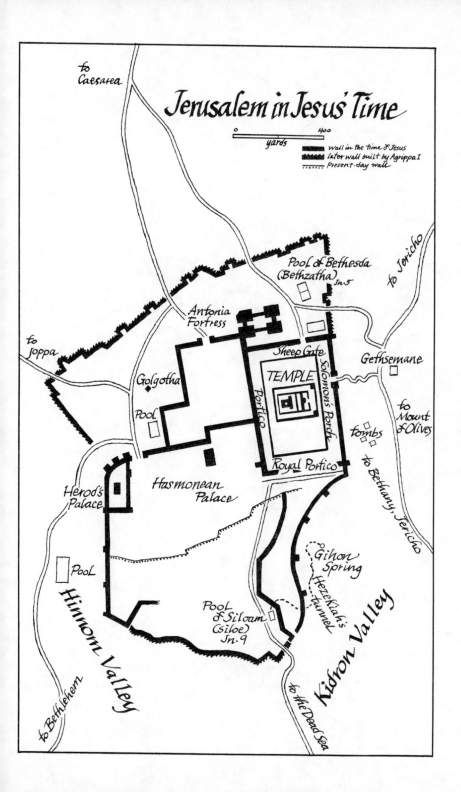

Jerusalem in Jesus' Time

0   yards   400

Wall in the time of Jesus
later wall built by Agrippa I
Present-day wall

to Caesarea

to Joppa

to Jericho

Pool of Bethesda (Bethzatha) Jn. 5

Antonia Fortress

Sheep Gate

Gethsemane

Golgotha

TEMPLE

Solomon's Porch

to Mount of Olives

Pool

Portico

tombs

to Bethany, Jericho

Royal Portico

Herod's Palace

Hasmonean Palace

Gihon Spring

Pool

Hezekiah's Tunnel

Hinnom Valley

Pool of Siloam (Siloe) Jn. 9

Kidron Valley

to Bethlehem

to the Dead Sea

1

The
Story and
Its Tellers

THIS BOOK IS ABOUT A MAN WHO TAUGHT HOLINESS AND GOD'S
supreme love, and lived them. He was a mystic at a time and place when
mysticism was not popular. He was a teacher in another mold than that of
the prevailing teachers. He was an outsider.

He was a Jew to the core of his being, yet not many Jews feel free to
hail him as one of their great ones. The Muslim world knows him from its
holy book, the Qur'an, but sketchily. He is a prophet to them, but not *the*
prophet. It is thought by many that his followers misconstrued him so
thoroughly—and Islam agrees in part with Judaism on this—that he has
been rendered almost useless as a teacher leading the way to God.

The worlds of China and India by and large do not know
him. Whenever the small number of those in touch with the West
come upon his teachings, they tend to respect them. As to the
miracles reported of him, the Hindu and the Buddhist are not put
off by them in the least. How else would a holy man have acted?
they ask.

His simplicity, his calm, his being at one with the world around him attracts not only the Hindu but the Taoist and the devotee of Zen as well. The disciple of Confucius recognizes wisdom when he sees it in any other master, so Jesus is no problem to one who follows Confucius.

Jesus has never been heard of by most of India's millions. If they know him at all, it is as the *avatara*, the God-expression acknowledged by most of the White world. That is generally enough to keep them from inquiring any further, in light of their experience of colonialism.

Black Africa is another matter. About one quarter of it is Christian—part in name and part in fact, which is the case with Christianity around the globe (one-third of the estimated 4.3 billion population is Christian). Africa's Christianity is undergoing a severe test in these days of rapid "indigenization." How this will come out is anybody's guess. Suffice it to say that the person of Jesus is so tied up with White colonialism and its low esteem for African values that it will be a marvel if Jesus manages to extricate himself on that continent from his friends—his Black African friends as much as his White.

Jesus is an important figure for a number of reasons. The larger question for any reader is: Is he significant for me?

It is already a preconception to say of Jesus that he is a holy man of great eminence. The record, however, seems to support the statement. Christians are convinced that he is the holiest of all humans. Since this is not true for other people—and since ranking the saints of the ages is a losing game—we are not going to get into it. Where would the world be without Gautama the Awakened One, without Moses or Hillel, without Lao Tzu or Muhammad? In the strictest sense possible, only God knows.

We have put our finger on something sensitive here. On the globe today, Jesus has probably never been more esteemed and Christianity never less. It is easy to toss off generalizations about the churches and to talk about hypocrisy or about using religion as a front for capitalism. Actually, the problem is not that easy to identify. It will not do to try to get back to the real Jesus and invite people to follow him, while letting the churches stew in their own juice. That is unrealistic. It is, in a sense, the solution of the healthy majority of Protestants (157 million total) in the world who call themselves Evangelicals, but in their rejection of all the churches, including the Protestant ones, they become a new church.

What seems real is to go in search of the heart of this Jewish hasid, this saint and son of God the churches revere, and see where it leads us. Whatever following him means to the various churches and who, exactly, he is to them is important, but that is the subject of other books, not this one. Only at the end, and briefly, will we explore the way Christians—and Muslims—now view him as an object of religious faith. This book is interested in the way five different communities of Christians (including the Pauline) believed in him toward the end of the first century.

There have been thousands of devotional books written about the life of Jesus, some of them good, some of them bad. Around the turn of this century, it began to come to light that you could not write a life of Jesus because none of the authors of the four gospels had written one. This stopped the learned from recounting his career in chronological sequence. No one else paid much attention. The romantics continued to explore Jesus' psychological states. Even the learned kept writing books about him, which they tended to title *Jesus*.

If the gospels were not biographies of Jesus, what were they? They were an attempt from four different viewpoints to help people share in the life of the one whom the early church believed in as "the Christ." The four whose gospels survive were convinced that Jesus still lived, not just in memory but in fact. Death had not held him. He was all life, human life suffused with the life of God. He had so powerfully proclaimed the word of God that many came to believe he *was* the word of God. They wrote their sketches of him in seeming biographical form as a way of sharing the life they were sure they possessed.

We say "they wrote them." To be sure, some four individuals did the work, and history has assigned them names. But things went differently regarding authorship in the ancient world. A person in a religious setting was not an author in quite the same way as now. If the writer was a Jew, he worked as part of a teaching band, a brotherhood.

Mark was the first of these community representatives to write. He made into one coherent narrative a variety of stories that had long been told about Jesus in the circles Mark traveled in. It was an artful performance, although the art did not show. What was especially remarkable was that Mark does not seem to have had any model. At least, nothing quite like a gospel has ever turned up from that period. The closest the Bible writing comes to the gospel type is the Elijah and Elisha cycles in the books of Kings, or the tales of Saul and David in the earlier books of Samuel. Philo, an Alexandrian Jew whose long life encompassed that of Jesus, wrote a life of Moses that was meant to be a biography but resembled a gospel in certain respects. Before him, numerous pagan authors had written biography-like accounts, among them Xenophon whose *Memorabilia* attempted to preserve the memory of Socrates from distortion, and a third-century B.C.E. author of a life of Alexander the Great, which we possess in fragments.

There was discovered in the desert sands of Egypt in 1945—as part of a late third-century library of Gnostic ("knowing" in the sense of "enlightened") Christians—a Gospel of Thomas. It is a very interesting and an important find, but it is not a gospel. It is a collection of Jesus' sayings. There is no narrative element, no story. That is essential to the notion of gospel. What Mark seems to have done, and done before anyone else, is to have taken elements of the story of Jesus' last days, which he had in his possession, and reworked them into a drama calculated to excite sympathy for him. Then, knowing how the end was going to come out, Mark arranged a variety of stories of what Jesus had said and done in such a way that they led up to his final arrest and sentence. Jesus' sufferings, death, and resurrection are climactic in Mark.

Mark had a collection of miracle stories in particular, the kinds of things we know were reported of other rabbis earlier and later in the century in which Jesus lived. Ḥoni (in Greek, Onias) the Circle-Maker and Ḥanina ben Dosa (whose father had the Greek name Dositheos, "gift of God") are the two best known. These were *ḥasidim*, as Jesus seems to have been, pious Jews. They were ordinary townsmen, not hermits or scholars, but gifted with special powers over nature. The word about such as these spread widely. It was said that their prayers were answered miraculously.

Mark's gospel reported numerous stories of struggle between Jesus and other religious teachers. That should not surprise us. The people who say they are serving God have always had trouble getting together on how to do it. There are also many tales in the gospels about ejecting demons or "unclean spirits" from innocent people troubled by them. The demons speak through people's mouths, showing a surprising knowledge of who Jesus is. They acknowledge his holiness and the power he exercises in God's name. It would all be fairly terrifying, like the stage effects in the film *The Exorcist*, except that Jesus seems able to silence them with a word. He never grows flustered or ill at ease. The Jesus of Mark is a man who replaces chaos with order, the turbulence of disease and frenzy with healed human life.

You might say that this is the pattern, the underlying theme of Mark's gospel. Jesus is the healer and in this sense the savior of humanity. He heals from what we we would call dementia and other psychoses, with always a strong indication of a more sinister influence. He heals from equally durable maladies that are still with us: paralysis, blindness, infectious disease. He brings people back from death (or apparent death; the difference does not greatly matter if the person is ready for burial). Whatever is inimical to human life and happiness, Jesus is set against in Mark's gospel. Mark wrote to defend against misunderstanding of the church's savior and to present a true image of him for disciples to follow. His gospel served as an account of origins for an early Christian community.

Matthew and Luke appear to possess collections of Jesus' sayings and stories that Mark does not have. If Mark portrayed him as a wonderworker, a "man from heaven" in control over nature, Matthew (in a gospel that some call a second edition of Mark) has remade Jesus in the image of the absolutely trustworthy teacher. This gospel is a legitimation of Jesus as teacher-legislator, with accompanying clues to interpret him in this role. Jesus' interpretation of the Torah, the books of Moses, is the only correct one for Matthew. The evangelist maintains that you can count on Jesus as a guide to perfect observance. Not the smallest part of a letter of the law is to be disregarded. There are signs of a great struggle in Matthew, not between demons and humans as in Mark, but between two parties of Jews. One, we assume, was the one that won out and became Judaism as we know it. It was the party of those sages led by Yoḥanan ben Zakkai who launched the corpus of practical decisions on the law that came to be set down in the year 200 of the Common Era as the Mishnah. The other party, the Matthew school, was, by a Yoḥanan standard, lax in its concern for *halakah* ("the way"), so much so that the emerging Judaism could not contain it. It became Christianity.

This second "way," like the first, did not view itself as a new religion. It thought it was Israel, an Israel made up of Jews and non-Jews, just as the covenant community that lived near the caves by the Dead Sea thought *it* was Israel. Jewish life in those times was full of tendencies and parties, movements and influences, none of which thought of itself as a "sect." Only the ultimate prevailing of Yoḥanan and the rabbis at Iavneh after 85 c.e. brought that about. Sects are defined by the prevailing parties or traditions that win out over them.

The large number of Judaism's gentile converts contributed immensely to Christianity's emergence as a daughter of Judaism. It continued to be interested in "proselytes" (a technical Jewish term rendered into that Greek word) long after rabbinic interest in them had waned. Far more influential on Christianity's emergence as a Jewish sect, however, was the predominance of the rabbis as claimants to the title of authentic interpreters of the meaning of Israel.

To speak of these things is to get ahead of our story. The third writer, Luke, besides possessing a collection of Jesus' sayings that Matthew had, knew and used Mark's gospel. He also had sources of his own, some of them on Jesus' teaching and activity, one in particular, perhaps, on his last days. Luke wrote a second book to follow up the life of the founder. Later history called it the Acts of the Apostles. It is a narrative of Jesus' successors and certain other disciples, told so as to indicate in Luke's time where the true tradition was to be found.

John is a special case. He has some of the historical reminiscences of the first three, but he uses them sparingly and always differently from the others. When it comes to his final chapters on Jesus' arrest, the inquiry into his offense, and his death, John seems to be following the same kinds of materials as Luke, not those of Mark and Matthew. Still, some think he followed Mark. John, too, writes to defend against a misunderstanding of the savior and to present a true picture of him. This evangelist tells Jesus' story as one of a revealer of God who comes down from heaven and has returned there. It, too, is a tale of origins for an early Christian community.

It used to be standard to say that the gospels were historically dependable in the descending order Mark, Matthew, Luke, John (which may be the order in which they were written). The last named got the lowest marks of all. Scholars do not hold that any more. They have come to learn that all four gospel writers were so deep in the business of audience persuasion that none gets very high marks for straight, unvarnished reporting. Each had an "angle, " and each seems to have received his component materials in a fairly well-developed condition. Whatever historical elements underlay these component parts, they had already been pretty well theologized by the time the evangelists came on them, a process they continued even further.

You can tell how all four put their special stamps on the data they received. So much is this the case that the view each gospel writer had of the meaning of Jesus is a much clearer matter than the state of his sources when he began to write.

We conclude these brief remarks on the various evangelists by saying that the fourth gospel is not as useless for facts on the life of Jesus as it once was thought to be, and leave it at that. John knows his Jewish life in Palestine better than the others, often better than Matthew. His sources in numerous matters are surprisingly dependable.

These pages are not meant to set the reader straight on history by telling "how it all happened." Some people care about that and some do not. There are books that explore the question admirably. The chapters that follow are going to look into who Jesus was and what he stood for in the eyes of those who first believed in him, which is another way of saying, from the viewpoints of the various evangelists. In other words, the gospels are going to be taken at face value as the late first-century accounts of faith in Jesus Christ that they are. No attempts will be made to establish, along the way, what he "really" said or did in his lifetime. Only occasionally will it be pointed out specifically that certain utterances of Jesus and narratives concerning him have to be acknowledged for what they are: theological developments of various early churches which convey what he meant in the lives of those believers. This is almost always the case in the gospels. The exceptions would be the relatively small amount of gospel material for which a case can be made that it happened in history just as reported.

2

The
Land and
Its People

THE HERO OF THE STORY OF JESUS IS, IN A WAY, THE LAND.
The *eretz Yisroel* is the hero because the Jewish people as a whole
and Jesus in particular cannot be understood apart from it. It was
sacred to them, but not merely because it was their homeland. That
kind of sacredness can be attributed to the soil of any people. Every
tribe, clan, or nation is fiercely attached to some portion of the
globe, which it would die to defend. A difference in the case of the
Jews—who are not unique in this—was the religious conviction
that Canaan had been deeded to them by their God. The soil was
holy with the holiness of YHWH (as they called him, without
pronouncing the name; in its place they said "the Name"). It would
retain this sacred character so long as they did not profane or
desecrate it by departing from the terms of their contract with
him. This contract they called a *b'rith*, a term we know better
as "covenant."

At circumcision on the eighth day after his birth, Jesus was made a "son of the covenant." At puberty, like any male Jew, he became what was called much later a "son of commandment," *bar mitzvah*. That meant that from infancy on he was attached to this corner of earth, this land, by a religious bond.

The land is the hero also because it has stayed faithful to God through successive plunder and restoration, reclamation and exhaustion. We are not speaking of these cyclic changes, however, so much as of the stability of places like Hermon and Tabor, Gerizim and Ebal, Carmel and Gilboa. They are still there, looking just as they did. So are the southern desert (Negev) and the northern, lyre-shaped lake (Kinnereth). The Judean wilderness remains, its gnarled rock surface still creased as it was by eruption a million years ago. The same stability marks the Jordan River, the Salt Sea, the Bay of Haifa. There are small changes, the things that water can do to a terrain, but the major features are largely as they were.

There are Jews everywhere in the land; that helps us to recognize it. They have been there since Abraham's time, some 3800 years ago. There are other Semites in the land, just as there were before the Hebrews came. These are no longer Canaanites and Moabites and Ammonites, but Arabs. These ancient tribes are a single people now, made so, paradoxically, by faith in Israel's God. They no longer call him Elohim, but Allah. The *ba'als* of the Canaanite high places are dead, but the one true God lives. He and the land.

This story is about a man, a Jew. The land has not left much trace of him—nothing like the memories strewn on the battle-grounds he knew as a boy: Megiddo, Esdraelon, Beit Shan. That may be because he was a man of peace. He died by execution and we know the site, or somewhere reasonably close to it. His growing-up place, Nazareth, has a single spring found near the town's main square. You can identify more than one site there as the brow of a hill from which some frenzied fellow-townspeople threatened to throw him, or so Luke tells it. There is the lake where he first recruited his fisherman associates in his venture of reform. On its shores are the ruins where Capernaum was and Bethsaida may have been. There is a thriving resort town at Tiberias, the site of one of the tombs of the medieval sage, Maimonides. Sidon in modern Lebanon is there to be visited, both as an excavated ruin and a modern town. So are Zarepath and Tyre.

The sandstone caves of his birthplace, Bethlehem, if indeed he was born there, are readily accessible. Nearby are the fields where David tended sheep. Since Bethlehem was David's home, it was the place where Jesus had to be born, in Luke's story of his origins. The Jericho road, which figures in one of Jesus' best-known tales, is very much to be seen. So is Bethany where he had an adult family of friends. There are two Jerichos. In the more recent one, where there is still a modern town, Jesus stayed with a runty tax-gouger named Zakkai. This Zacchaeus got religion the day Jesus visited him. Jesus spoke to him of "being a son of Abraham" and of "salvation" as if they were the same. Encounters like that happened with any number of people during his brief career. Some of these ended badly, just as he did. From the fragmentary reports we have, people did not seem to care.

The one site in Jerusalem with which Jesus was most closely identified, the temple area, is not in Jewish hands except for the "western wall" at its base. The Muslims have it. You find many paradoxes like that in this land. There are the fortresses of Ṣur and 'Akko (ancient Tyre and Ptolemais), where the crusaders proclaimed a bloody kingship in his name. The walls are thick beyond belief; the unsupported, vaulted ceilings masterpieces of medieval skill. The woeful paradox is that there was slaughter in his name.

One senses the same paradox in Caesarea, the coastal ruin south of Akko. Pontius Pilate used to stay there as much as he could to avoid the stresses and the heavy atmosphere of Jerusalem. There is an aqueduct there, an outdoor theater, and various large impressive ruins. What imperative of power made Pilate feel he had to finish off the Galilean teacher? It did not make sense. But then, none of the judicial murders of history do. A kind of madness seizes humanity, impelling it to kill its great ones.

The Church of the Holy Sepulchre, built over the Hill of the Skull where Jesus died, is still a place of pious turbulence. The calm of Caesarea with its handsome view of the Mediterranean puts the question of Jesus better, somehow. What threat to imperial safety could the Nazarene have been in Pilate's eyes from sixty miles away, southeast across the Carmel range? What were Pilate's thoughts as he left this seaside calm one spring day to head for

Jerusalem and the Passover? Apprehension, surely, at the mood of
the times. Had he any inkling of the existence of the teacher from
Nazareth?

An old proverb likens a fortuitous occurrence to "the way
Pilate got into the creed." This man who was a stereotype of military cruelty got into the liturgical formularies of the Christians
because events were dated by the terms of imperial officials. It was
as simple as that. In light of subsequent happenings, though, it was
not that simple at all. The gospel writers made him an unwilling
hero and the church has been burdened with him ever since.

Regionalism ran strong in the land that was sanctified by a
holy God. We have no reason to suppose that Jesus was uninfluenced by the regional spirit. He was not just a Palestinian Jew, he
was a Galilean Jew. Another way to say that is to describe him as a
non-Judean Jew. He was from the homeland but not the heartland.
Yet he seems to have been a Jew committed to fellow Jews, even exclusively, as Matthew tells it: "My mission is only to the lost sheep
of the house of Israel."[1]

The tribal structure of early times, when Benjamin and
Judah (together known as "Judah") inhabited the south and the
other ten tribes ("Israel" or "Ephraim") the north, had largely disin-
tegrated by the Roman period. People knew who they were by tribe
as Americans might know themselves to be those whose forebears
came from a certain place in Slovakia. But, in the main, the pattern
of actual settlement by tribe was long forgotten. The reminiscence
on Jesus was that he was of David's tribe, Judah. Hillel, too, the
great rabbi of the lifetime before Jesus, was sprung from David.
Saul of Tarsus knew that the neighboring tribe of Benjamin claimed
him. This kind of information was by no means unusual. Middle
Eastern peoples have long memories for such details.

We need not suppose that Jesus' distant family origins in the
south exerted any great pull on him. Nothing is recorded, at least,
that would indicate this. When he came to prominence, the fact
that Galilee was his homeplace was raised against any pretensions
he might have had to prophetic status: " 'Do not tell us you are a
Galilean too,' they taunted him. 'Look it up. You will not find the
Prophet coming from Galilee.' "[2]

---

1. Mt 15:24   2. Jn 7:52

There is a good possibility that this exchange was composed long after the fact to convey the poor view that the south had of northerners, but it has the ring of authenticity to it. So does the remark attributed to certain bystanders after they heard a servant girl say of Peter, on the night Jesus was arrested, that he was of Jesus' company: "You are certainly one of them! Even your accent gives you away!"[3] As reported, the remark is neutral enough, but the conventional outlook of the Jerusalemites of the time was that the Galilean dialect was the speech of rustics. The region itself was thought by the learned to be more than half heathen. The very name Galilee is the first part of a longer phrase, "the arc-shaped region (*galil*) of the gentiles." Even in Jesus' time, non-Jews probably predominated there.

A slur against Jesus' hometown appears in the fourth gospel: "Can anything good come from Nazareth?"[4] We might put the remark down to local folk wisdom. Yet we know that *notsri* ("Nazarene") became the ordinary designation for a Christian. This could have meant that the town name had entered into the easy vocabulary of opprobrium from the Jewish side, just as nowadays people in anger call others "nazis" or "commies." The gospel writer John may have been recording the later struggle rather than the situation in Jesus' lifetime. Or the explanation could be simpler: identifying Jesus' followers in a neutral way by his place of origin.

Nazareth was not sufficiently distinguished to come in for a single mention in the Bible. Its northern neighbor Sfad, likewise not mentioned, eclipsed it in every way. The emperor's lakeshore resort town, Tiberias, similarly far outshone the town that the gospels bring to prominence as Jesus' adult home, Capernaum.

Popular disdain for Galilee and its inhabitants is well attested to outside the gospels. Much later, from the second century to the fourth, Tiberias on the lake it gave its name to (otherwise the Sea of Galilee or Lake Kinnereth) was to be important as the place where the Mishnah and the Gemara were written—the earliest collections of rabbinic commentary on the Bible—and the Palestinian Talmud codified. But all that lay ahead. In Jesus' day Galileans were thought by a Judean standard to be lax in observance of the

---

3. Mt 26:73   4. Jn 1:46

law. Jesus seems to have confirmed the worst suspicions of the more sophisticated Jerusalemites.

The differences between the two regions were economic in good part. That is often the case in such rivalries. One need only recall the resentment of the United States harbored by many Europeans. Europeans possess culture, the arts, the libraries; Americans are merely rich and vulgar. The imbalance between natural resources plus a unifying tongue, and a continent that is a geographic and linguistic patchwork, cries out for an explanation. This the peoples of Europe are quick to supply.

Things were much the same, on a smaller scale, in Palestine. Galilee was rich in resources, like Minnesota. The claim of a religious and intellectual superiority was made for hardscrabble Judea, if only to satisfy the psyche of its inhabitants. Judea was bound to despise fishermen since its dried-up wadis and its Salt Sea could not produce a single minnow. The same was true of trade routes. Galilee had them in both directions, north-south and east-west. Jerusalem was a capital that lay on the banks of no river whatever. She had to fall back on Har Zion, the sacred mountain, to provide her with greatness. Even John on the banks of the Jordan and the holy men of the Judean desert alongside the Dead Sea made a kind of sense to the rabbis of Judea. Their land literally breathed religion. The soil of Galilee, the stupid giant to the north, was devoid of it.

Well, not entirely. There was one commodity that Galilee was abundantly supplied with, and that was patriotism. And patriotism by definition sprang in the Jewish culture from religious conviction. The south was none too pleased with the violent forms patriotism took in the north. That was the case, at least, in two orbits of Jewish leadership and for two quite different reasons. The Sadducees and the sons of Boethus (the Jewish historian Josephus tells us), two wings of the aristocratic priestly class, had made their peace with Rome. As collaborators with the occupying régime, they were not looking for any trouble from zealous hotheads out to destroy the uneasy balance. The deeply religious Pharisees opposed the violent overtures for a better reason. Their policy was the one Jeremiah had counseled centuries before in the face of the Assyrian threat. The Pharisees favored letting history take its course while they placed all their trust in the LORD. He would protect them. They

were convinced that the perfect fidelity to the law they taught
would please the LORD as nothing else could. He had made his demands of Israel on Sinai. They taught the rightness of fulfilling
them.

Do we have any evidence that Jesus was part of the Zealot
movement in its violent expression? There are strong indications
that some associated with it attached themselves to him. One of the
two Simons in his immediate following was designated "the
Zealot." Jesus' closest friends went armed. On one occasion some
are described as brandishing the knives they wore at their sides.
These could have been fishing knives, but that is not the point.

There has been some guesswork that "Iscariot," the designation of one of the two Judases, and "Barjonah," a name of Simon,
better known as Peter, are words that had some association with
violence. The speculation is not conclusive however.

An armed insurrectionist in those days was called in Greek a
lēistēs (though the word could also mean a simple brigand). The
phenomenon was so widespread that it became a loanword in
Hebrew, listis. Jesus is spoken of as having been crucified between
two of them. The gospels retain a story of a bargain offered by
Pilate to spare Jesus' life in preference to that of another such in-
surgent. Almost certainly Jesus died on a charge of complicity in an
uprising against Rome. The title placed over his head on the cross
called him mockingly, "The king of Judea [lit., the Judeans]."

The trouble with all this circumstantial evidence is that one
must disregard all of Jesus' recorded utterances to make the case for
his interest in armed revolt.

This has not kept some from doing it. The result is a theorizing not so much by inference as by inversion. The evangelists must
be made conspirators—men who transformed the image of Jesus
totally—in order to see in him a violent man. A German scholar,
Samuel Reimarus (d. 1768), was the first to do this. The end is
nowhere in sight. One cannot but be reminded that Jesus accused
those who attributed his works to Satan of blasphemy against the
holy spirit.[5]

We are told what he said about peace: "Happy are the
peacemakers; they shall be called children of God," and:

---

5. Mk 3:28–30

Whoever grows angry with his brother shall be liable to judgment; anyone who uses abusive language toward his brother shall be answerable to the Sanhedrin; if he holds him in contempt he risks the fires of Gehenna. If you bring your gift to the altar and there recall that your brother has anything against you, leave your gift at the altar, go first to be reconciled to your brother, and then come and offer your gift.[6]

That is not the language of a violent man. It is not even the speech of one who so hates sin that he is at ease with hating the enemies of God.

Jesus said once to a friend who used violence to protect him: "Put back your sword where it belongs. Those who use the sword are sooner or later destroyed by it."[7] In another gospel Jesus counsels buying a sword in a context of instructing his disciples about the hostility they will encounter.[8] But when they take him literally he snorts impatiently. It is in this same gospel that he heals the victim of his friends' impetuous swordplay.

He had enough of the Galilean spirit, however, that he was not totally passive. The one authentically violent act attributed to him sprang from his zeal for God's house:

When they reached Jerusalem he entered the temple precincts and began to drive out those who were buying and selling. He overturned the moneychangers' table and the stalls of those selling doves; moreover, he would not permit anyone to carry things through the temple area.[9]

That action identifies Jesus as a man of passion. In the mold of the prophets, he resists fiercely the abuse of true religion. He does not simply resist the fact of commerce, which, after all, is being carried on in the outer court, the designated place for it. The prophet Jeremiah had charged that some in his time made the temple a "brigands' cave," a place of sanctuary after their violent deeds. Jesus makes the same charge: They cloaked destructive careers—every sort of evil—with a mantle of religion.

To extrapolate from that one outburst of Jesus to a mentality of armed resistance to the Romans is, however, perverse. His

---

6. Mt 5:9; 5:22–24   7. Mt 26:52   8. Lk 22:36, 51   9. Mk 11:15–16

real target is not "thieves" but "brigands" (lēistōn). He opposes those who say that violence is the business of religion. One is reminded of the attitude abroad in this country a short while back that could lump the destruction of draft records with the carpet-bombing of Vietnam, calling both "violence." The charge was perverse.

Jesus may have had the Galilean temperament, if there was such a thing; he seems to have kept it in check. His tongue was quick, but there is nothing of the hotheadedness about him of a Peter or a James and John, the "sons of thunder." He said he came to light a fire on the earth[10] as Elijah did, to bring not peace but a sword.[11] The blaze turns out to be one of zeal for the true God. The divisiveness is between members of a household as they set the priority of their allegiances in order. Neither Herod's palace nor the Roman fortress Antonia was ever the target of Jesus' metaphoric fire and sword. For Herod he had but one word of contempt, "that fox."

Two regions have been featured up to this point: Judea, the home of intellect and speech, and Galilee, the center of mindless plots.

There was a third region, Samaria—modern Shom'ron. It stood between north and south like a changeling, a goose among swans. A brief tale told by Jesus has had the effect of prefixing "good" to Samaritan, causing the people of that region to be thought of as natural-born helpers in distress.[12] A cured leper, the one of ten who expressed gratitude, is also a Samaritan, to reinforce the image.[13] An unsophisticated female inquirer at Jacob's well near Shechem is a member of this people.[14]

Who were the Samaritans, that Jews in general thought ill of them while Christians fell into the opposite stereotype?

They started out as Jews caught in a cultural backwater— more accurately, a mountain fastness. They were a people that the march of history had passed by. In ancient times their land had been inhabited by the "half-tribe" of Manasseh, son of Joseph. Their chief shrine was at Shechem where Joshua, at the end of the

---

10. See Lk 12:49   11. See Mt 10:34   12. See Lk 10:30-37
13. See Lk 17:16   14. See Jn 4:4-42

completed conquest of Canaan, made a final covenant with the people, setting up a memorial pillar to mark the event.[15] Shechem lay slightly to the east of the notch made by Mt. Gerizim and Mt. Ebal. It was a sanctuary of early importance. Mt. Gerizim was a mount of blessing (that is, fit for Israelite sacrifice), Mt. Ebal one of cursing (that is, unfit).[16] Shechem-Gerizim, in a word, was a place where God would clearly put his name.

A funny thing happened on the way to the first temple. David defeated everyone in sight and founded Jerusalem. Solomon consolidated his father's gains and made the temple he built the one true shrine of Israelite faith. Prescriptive possession won a round over history, as it often does.

The Samarians began to be thought of as outlaws, whereas in fact they were only northern losers. They kept appealing to their scriptures, the same books of Moses the Judeans had, against the humiliating fact of defeat.

The Judeans countered the claim to Gerizim as the one God-designated shrine by altering the holy books in two places. They wrote in "Mt. Ebal" where the whole tenor of the passages requires "Mt. Gerizim."[17] Such was the penalty the Samarians paid for their religious conservatism, for not going along with an accomplished political fact. Their challenge to Mt. Zion as the only true shrine led to their expulsion (or secession, depending on how you look at it) around 332 B.C.E. when they let Alexander the Great build them a temple on Gerizim.[18] The second-century B.C.E. book of Sirach throws a characteristic Jewish brickbat at the Samaritans, as they had then become, a separate religious people:

My whole being loathes two nations,
   The third is not even a people:
Those who live in Seir and Philistia,
   And the degenerate people who live at Shechem.[19]

Jesus, who always wore the mantle of reconciler, seems to have attempted to reconcile the Samaritans with the Jews. It could not have helped his image. Witness, for example: "Are we not

---

15. See Jos 24:26–28   16. See Dt 11:29; 27:11–13   17. See Dt 27:4 and Jos 8:30
18. See Neh 13:28–30 for the event that probably marked it.   19. Sir 50:25–26

right, after all, in saying you are a Samaritan, and possessed besides?"[20] He denied the charge of possession and disregarded the other of being a Samaritan. It was like a fair-minded person being called nowadays a "nigger-lover" or someone who hung out with Jews. He would have delighted in the attribution, and been equally delighted that his later followers numbered Samaritans of their company.

This was a man of a particular region of Palestine who did not think regionally. He thought that salvation was of "the Jews," writes John, the people of the region south of Samaria with whom the Galileans identified. Yet he spoke and acted as if it did not stop there.

We are told that in a few brief excursions he went beyond Jewish borders.

He acted throughout his short public life as if the blessings of the Torah were not meant to stop at the border—any border.

---

20. Jn 8:48

3

The
Sages and
the Separated

JESUS CANNOT BE ANALYZED IN HIS SUCCESSES AND HIS failures as the world reckons these matters. This can no more be done than it can be learned why the Buddha was largely ignored in the religious life of his own country, India, but accepted enthusiastically in countries to the east and southeast. The fairly vigorous Jewish and Christian communities of the Arabian peninsula in the seventh century that yielded to the religion of Islam provide another such subject for speculation. Why were they absorbed into Islam? We may speculate but it will be fruitless.

Jesus was a recognizable figure of his time, a pious man of whom numerous miracles are reported. He was at the same time an itinerant teacher committed to the restoration of Jewish life under the law. He seems to have had a tenuous relation to the baptizing sects. Although he was from Galilee—liberation country—Jesus was apparently free of the violent zeal that marked his compatriots.

He did not focus on the temple as the holiest place in the nation. He seemed to concentrate on human attitudes apart from any considerations of space or place.

One important matter was the supposed failure of Jesus to show interest in the so-called oral law. This was the tradition of practical decisions on day-to-day conduct in conformity with the five books of Moses, writings that the Babylonian exile had made central in Jewish life. The Dead Sea community has left us scrolls which indicate that, while passionately devoted to the law and the prophets, the community members were no more concerned with rabbinic decisions than Jesus was. Something else he had in common with the Dead Sea communities was an outlook about the "final age," although he did not use the full apocalyptic vocabulary of the group at Qumrân. Another seeming failure of great magnitude was the opposition the gospels say he incurred—indeed invited—from a group called the Pharisees. If he treated these men in his lifetime as the gospels report it, we should not be surprised that his memory did not live in honor in Judaism. Their intellectual descendants, after all, were the rabbis whose wisdom led to the writings that are the backbone of modern Judaism.

On a first reading of the gospels, we find that a mysterious coalition of "scribes and Pharisees" seems to dog Jesus' steps at every turn. He is not gentle with them. He does not try to understand them, but goes on the assumption that they are acting in bad faith. In the fourth gospel, John substitutes "the Jews" ("the Judeans"?) for "the scribes and Pharisees." The term seems to describe the same antagonists. But this usage of John is puzzling in a situation where practically everyone was a Jew. It would be as if a consistent, hostile dialogue were carried on in France between Joan of Arc and "the French."

We should see what kind of exchanges are reported before we try to discover who was involved:

Some of the scribes were sitting there asking themselves: "Why does the man talk that way?"[1] . . . When the scribes of the Pharisees saw that he was eating with tax gatherers and sinners [viz., offenders against the law], they complained to

1. Mk 2:6–7

his disciples: "Why does he eat with such as these?"[2]. . . At this [his disciples' pulling off heads of grain as they went along], the Pharisees protested: "Look! why do they do a thing not permitted on the sabbath?"[3]. . . When the Pharisees went outside they immediately began to plot with the Herodians how they might destroy him.[4] . . . The Pharisees and some of the experts in the law who had come from Jerusalem gathered around him. They had observed a few of his disciples eating meals without having purified—that is, washed—their hands. . . So they questioned him: "Why do your disciples not follow the traditions of our ancestors. . . ?"[5] The Pharisees came forward and began to argue with him. They were looking for some heavenly sign from him as a test. . . .[6] When he instructed the disciples, "Keep your eyes open! Be on guard against the yeast of the Pharisees and the yeast of Herod," they concluded among themselves that it was because they had no bread. . . .[7] They put him this question: "Why do the scribes claim that Elijah must come first?"[8] Then some Pharisees came up and as a test began to ask him whether it was permissible for a husband to divorce his wife.[9]

These passages are all taken from Mark, the first gospel to be written. He seems to think that Pharisees and scribes are two different groups, the second a sub-set of the first. Overall, he is fairly careful about his nomenclature of antipathy to Jesus, whether or not he understands the various groups he finds mentioned in his sources. The other three gospels are progressively less careful. Some of the worst bitterness reported between Jesus and the Pharisees does not appear above. For example, in Matthew, Jesus often calls them hypocrites, a word for an actor borrowed from the Greeks by the Jews who had no living theater.[10] He accuses them of putting human traditions in place of God's commandments, thereby nullifying God's word in favor of the doctrine they have devised and handed on.[11] The much stronger language of Matthew reaches a crescendo in Chapter 23:

---

2. Mk 2:16   3. Mk 2:24   4. Mk 3:6; see 12:13   5. Mk 7:1-2, 5
6. Mk 8:11   7. Mk 8:15-16   8. Mk 9:11   9. Mk 10:2
10. Mt 7:5   11. See Mk 7:8-13

Blind guides! You strain out the gnat and swallow the camel.
Woe to you scribes and Pharisees, you frauds! You cleanse
the outside of cup and dish and leave the inside filled with lust
and loot.[12]

A series of six maledictions or "Woes" is heaped on them, some of
the gentler titles employed being "sons of the murderers of the
prophets," "nests of vipers," and "serpents' brood."[13] This material
could have been originally a catalogue of obloquy by Christian
prophets against their opponents which did not contain mention of
the scribes and Pharisees. The target group would have been added
by Matthew and Luke or their source.

The Jewish *sopher* or scribe was someone learned in the law
without regard to partisan allegiance. The best-known of the early
scribes, a certain Sirach, wrote a book about conduct that his
grandson Yeshua (Jesus) translated into Greek. The scribes in the
time of Jesus of Nazareth later came to be known as Pharisees, a
fact which Mark, who sets the terminology, does not seem to
know. The priestly group, the Sadducees, were not interested in the
development of the oral law. When ultimately naming the conspirators against Jesus' life, Mark eliminates the Pharisees, even
though he had identified them as early plotters. In the event he im-
plicates a coalition of elders, chief priests, and scribes.[14] This seems
to indicate that he is relying on a "passion source" that does not
name the Pharisees.

At times a scribe will be in admiration of Jesus' teaching and
Jesus of his.[15] At other times representatives of this class are spoken
of as ostentatious and hypocritical, almost as if by definition.[16]

The scribes arose in the time of Ezra, the postexilic priest-
reformer who flourished around 400 B.C.E. Originally they seem to
have been transmitters of the Torah, not only in written form but
in the law courts as well. They had to suggest passages of the Torah
applicable to the case being tried. This made them interpreters, not
just copyists. Ambiguity marked many passages in the scriptures,
while other passages could not be adhered to because of the

---

12. Mt 23:24–25   13. Mt 23:31, 33
14. See Mk 8:31; 10:33; 11:18, 27; 14:1, 10, 43, 53; 15:1
15. See Mk 12:32–34   16. See Mk 12:38–40

changes brought about by time. The "words of the scribes" thus became as binding as the Torah but always conservatively; the sacred text was appealed to directly in every instance. Interpretation, in other words, remained a matter of code law, not case law. The scribal profession marshalled the arguments. It eventually moved into the whole field of civil and criminal law.

The scribes continued to exist as men of the law but they were gradually superseded in influence by the "sages" (ḥakamim). These searchers after wisdom looked for ways to hold out the possibility of uninterrupted ritual purity under the law. Cleanliness was to be a matter not of priests or of sacred areas only, but of wherever there were Jews. A hedge of interpretation was built around the Torah, meaning that wherever the Jew was, there separation from a defiling environment could be achieved. Since the movement made possible ritual holiness for all with ethical excellence as its concomitant, it must be described as "popular." The movement was not intended to be a party. It was meant to be Israel itself. The ḥakamim attempted to build up a solid tradition of cases in which doubts about how to keep the law were settled. Ultimately the Torah was adhered to, but a great body of decisions and precedents was the intermediary between it and the people.

No aspersions should be cast on this effort; rather the contrary. Its goal was the Torah for everyone. Two things of great consequence about the movement cannot be settled finally. One is the exact relation of these wise men (whose existence we know of from the late second century B.C.E. onward) and a class known as the p'rushim. The other is the relation between the Pharisees of the gospels and both ḥakamim (sages) and p'rushim. The latter term ordinarily means the "separated." If it does in this case, the question is, separated from what or whom? It can also mean "those who distinguish" or "the precisionists." If such was its meaning, what was its history?

As far as we can tell, the term at first had a good sense: the holy who became such by separation from defilement. Then it acquired a less attractive meaning: those who were separated from the "people of the land," the peasantry careless about the obligations of the oral Torah. In post-Christian times this scorn for the unenlightened comes into prominence in Jewish sources. There are already indications of it in the gospels.

In reading the gospels we will be wise to understand "Pharisee" in its earlier sense of someone interested in holiness for all, unless the contrary is indicated. Luke tells the story of a Pharisee who has Jesus as his house guest and proceeds to have an honest difficulty over Jesus' physical contact with a woman known to be a sinner.[17] Another time Luke describes a friendly delegation of Pharisees who try to keep Jesus out of the clutches of Herod, the ruler of Galilee.[18]

The norm for a proper modern understanding of this term is not the disposition of Pharisees toward Jesus but the recognition of a genuine desire on the part of Pharisees to see that ritual purity was observed. Jesus (or the gospel writers) went on record in their day as to where good will—or its absence—lay. Usually, it is not hard to learn whether the specific groups of Pharisees mentioned in the gospels are well-intentioned men of legal wisdom or imposers of burdens on the common people. Since references to the latter predominate, this is unfortunately the characterization that has survived. It may not have been the prevailing one in Jesus' day.

The Talmud is the literary product of the descendants of the sages, who are, in effect, the "Pharisees" referred to by the historian Josephus and the New Testament. Yet the Talmud often speaks as unfavorably of the Separated as the gospels do of the "Pharisees." This attack on its own spiritual forebears would constitute a puzzle if it were not for the fact that the simple identification of the Separated with overscrupulous observants seems overfacile and even downright false.

Thus, the Babylonian and Palestinian Talmuds both speak of the "wounds" or "blows" of the Separated. They classify these interpreters into seven types.[19] Five seem to be unfavorable designations and two favorable. The latter speak of the p'rush as one who fears like Job or loves like Abraham, "our father who made the evil inclination good." The first five types are described as anxious to keep the law in such a way that the talmudic authors can only be holding them up to ridicule. There is thus the p'rush of

---

17. See Lk 7:36-40   18. See Lk 13:31
19. See B. Sotah 22a, b (Babylonian Talmud); B. Berakoth 9, 5 and J. Sotah 5, 5 (Palestinian Talmud)

Shechem who carries the commandments on his shoulders, and the knee-knocking *p'rush* who says, "Spare me a moment and I will fulfill my obligation." Others are those who balance sin against commandment (in the Babylonian Talmud they rub themselves against the walls to draw blood); those bent over like a pestle in a mortar for crushing herbs; those who say in the Palestinian Talmud: "From the little that belongs to me I will give up some to fulfill a command"; and the type that asks: "What further duty is there for me that I may perform it?"

The irony intended in these five classifications is clear. The Job-like fear and Abrahamic love praised in the other two are equally evident in the scribe to whom Jesus says: "You are not far from the rule of God."[20] King Yannai (Alexander Janneus, who died in 76 B.C.E.) said to his wife on his deathbed: "Do not fear either the *p'rushim* or the non-*p'rushim* but the hypocrites who ape the *p'rushim*. They act like Zimri but expect a reward like Phinehas." He was referring to a usurper of the kingship of Israel, Zimri, in 885 B.C.E.,[21] and to Aaron's grandson through Eleazar, Phinehas,[22] who much earlier was given the pledge of an everlasting priesthood as a reward.[23]

Jesus, like the dying king Janneus, had no difficulty whatever with the genuine article, the sage who sought holiness in observance of the law. He was an opponent of the counterfeit types recorded in the Talmud. Unfortunately his reported teaching has kept the latter stereotype alive while not providing an equally vivid picture of the Separated who are such out of love, like Abraham.

Recent years have witnessed attempts to rehabilitate the Pharisees, even to glorify them. Unfortunately we do not have enough evidence from the period to do either of these things safely. We are on firmer ground in supposing that the gospel rhetoric against them describes only some, as is the case in any age with doctors, lawyers, or the clergy. The strong language of Jesus (or Matthew) is fated to remain. Note, however, the distinction it contains:

The scribes and the Pharisees have succeeded Moses as teachers: therefore do and observe everything they tell you

---

20. Mk 12:34   21. See 1 Kgs 16:8–20   22. See Ex 6:25   23. See Nm 25:13

but do not follow their example. Their words are bold but their deeds are few. They bind up heavy loads, hard to carry, and lay them on other men's shoulders while they themselves will not lift a finger to budge them. All their works are performed to be seen. They widen their phylacteries [leather cartridges on wrist and forehead containing scripture] and wear huge tassels. They are fond of places of honor at banquets and the front seats in synagogues, of marks of respect in public and being called Rabbi.[24]

Matthew slips imperceptibly at this point into strictures against the title "Rabbi" and the use of "Teacher" and "Father." He wishes to restrict the first two to Jesus, the last to God, doubtless because such honorific titles characterize his religious opponents. His counsel has not been nearly as seriously taken as his castigation of the Pharisees. Yet all are of a piece.

The gospel language against the Pharisees is so strong that Christianity is in the position of having set Jesus the Jewish teacher against all his contemporaries who claimed learning in the law. The opposition is unfortunate. The verdict of the gospels on the scribes and Pharisees, like that of Jewish sources, more closely approximates the general verdict that can be leveled against all humanity: There are all sorts.

---

24. Mt 23:2–7

4

The
Wise Man

Part of the difficulty in writing about Jesus is that we do not have good contemporary sources about Jewish life in his time. Aside from the gospels and the Dead Sea scrolls, there are only two Jewish writers of the period whose work remains: Flavius Josephus, a Graeco-Roman-type historian who was born shortly after Jesus died, and Philo, a philosopher of Alexandria who was born well before Jesus and died after him.

A more serious problem is to relate the record we possess on Jesus to the record of Jewish life in 70 c.e. Some of the rabbinic literature, like the *Sayings of the Fathers*, is quite early in its date of composition. Much that occurs in the Mishnah and some of the Talmud goes back to well before Jesus' time. If something is reported of a saint or a sage who, we are sure, clearly lived before his time, what is attributed *could* have preceded Jesus. We then have a good lead concerning Jesus' antecedents, even if we do not have historical certainty. The trouble is, it is hard to tell exactly who and what influenced Jesus, whether in the way of piety, wisdom, or wonderworking.

The reader who knows the Jewish mystical tradition may wonder why little account has been taken of it in the story of one who experienced God as Jesus did. For indeed, *merkabah* mysticism (the "chariot") was part of the heritage of the early rabbis. The mystical tradition was derived from the early visionary chapters of Ezekiel, especially 1 and 10, as a basis for contemplation and experience. The Mishnah contains in one place a prohibition against reading "the chapter of the Chariot"[1] and in another this caution: "The Chariot may not be interpreted before a person alone, unless he is one of the Wise who possess understanding based on knowledge."[2]

The innovator Yoḥanan ben Zakkai, great leader of the reconstructed Jewish community of learning after the fall of Jerusalem in 70 C.E., was apparently affected somewhat by the trend toward seeking the experience of awe in the awesomeness of God. Later the rabbis tried to bring mysticism under control but, as with the young man who was deemed unfit for the ministry because cheerfulness kept breaking in, Jewish mysticism flourished apart from any such control.

The same may be said of the apocalyptic eschatology we shall be discussing in Chapter 8. Much of this writing has not survived in Jewish circles because of a language principle: it was preserved in Greek and the rabbis were committed to Hebrew. The writing was, moreover, too fanciful or poetic for certain tastes, and too little concerned with achieving holiness through observance of the law. Yet it would be a mistake to suppose that all remembrance of the apocalyptic tradition faded, or even that it found no sympathetic place in the Mishnah and later in the Talmud. It is one of the virtues of Judaic tradition that it never forgets any place its people have been.

With which elements in Jewish life did Jesus resonate most? We have the record of only two other traditions, the Essene and the rabbinic. One peaked before, one after, his time. He was not

---

1. *Megillah* 4, 10   2. *Hagigah* 2, 1

especially close to either. Yet, Jesus should not be thought of as "offbeat" in his religious concerns. He was simply marching to a different drummer in a parade where no drummer was "official."

When Jesus of Nazareth, wonderworker and mystic, opened his mouth to teach, however, he was solidly in the wisdom tradition. In its origins it had come to Israel from Egypt and Babylonia. The wise sayings were originally advice to the upper, nonworking classes on how to keep their advantaged position in society. Lord Chesterfield's letters to his son may serve as an example: a respectable ethical ideal for "upstairs" without much hint of the existence of a "downstairs." Gradually, the pithy utterances of Jewish wisdom literature became more elevated in tone. From counsel on avoiding harlots and failure in business (given for roughly the same reasons), the proverbs moved into the highest ethical and religious spheres. They did not leave behind entirely, however, the homey counsel of their origins. Thus, the author Sirach could write the following in immediate juxtaposition, the first passage coming after the second:

> As the rising of the sun is clear to all,
>   so the glory of the LORD fills all his works;
> Yet even God's holy ones must fail
>   in recounting the wonders of the LORD,
> Though God has given these, his hosts, the strength
>   to stand firm before his glory. . . .[3]

> Keep a close watch on your daughter,
>   lest she make you the sport of your enemies. . . .
> See that there is no lattice in her room,
>   no place overlooking approaches to the house.
> Let her not parade her charms before men,
>   or spend her time with married women;
> For just as moths come from garments,
>   so harm to women comes from women.[4]

Jesus would have been able to converse freely with this Sirach, the purveyor of the wisdom tradition two centuries before, who concentrated on the literary genre of the wise saying, the

---

3. Sir 42:16–17   4. Sir 42:11–13

packaged insight that hoped to make its point through riddle, paradox, and maxim. Sirach was a *sopher*, an intellectual. He was somewhat pompous but terribly earnest. Looking back over his life's experience, he made a collection of helpful generalizations for the guidance of youth.

He wrote at one point "in praise of famous men":

> Like a fire there appeared the prophet
>   whose words were as a flaming furnace.
> Their staff of bread he shattered,
>   in his zeal he reduced them to straits. . . .
> How awesome are you, Elijah.
>   Whose glory is equal to yours?
> You brought a dead man back to life from the
>   nether world, by the will of the LORD. . . .
> You are destined, it is written, in time to come
>   to put an end to wrath before the day of the LORD. . . .
> Then Elisha, filled with a twofold portion of
>   his spirit, wrought many marvels merely by his word.
> During his lifetime he feared no one,
>   nor could any man intimidate his will.
> Nothing was beyond his power;
>   beneath him flesh was brought back to life.
> In life he performed wonders
>   and, after death, marvelous deeds.[5]

Sirach had no special institutional problems with the Aaronide priesthood or with keeping Moses' law. He took both for granted as legitimate aspects of Jewish life. He has unstinted praise for Moses the lawgiver but perhaps more for Aaron the priest:

> For Moses ordained him [Aaron] and anointed him with
>   holy oil
> In a covenant with him and with his family,
>   as permanent as the heavens,
> That he would serve God in his priesthood
>   and bless his people in his name. . . .
> He gave to him his laws, and authority to

5. Sir 48:1–14 *passim*

prescribe and to judge,
To teach the precepts to his people
    and the ritual to the descendants of Israel.[6]

    The medium of this author, we have said, was the wise saying. Here are a few of the many in his storehouse:

The shoot of violence will not flourish,
    for the root of the godless is on rock. . . .[7]

If you are chosen to preside at a dinner,
    do not be puffed up
    but be with the guests as one of them;
Take care of them first before you sit down. . . .[8]

For the sake of profit many sin,
    and the struggle for wealth blinds the eyes.
Like a peg driven between fitted stones,
    between buying and selling is sin wedged in.[9]

    Many of his sayings are like those on which Jesus patterned his:

Least is the bee among winged things
    but she reaps the choicest of harvests. . . .[10]

To the poor man extend your hand,
    that your blessing may be complete. . . .
Avoid not those who weep
    but mourn with those who mourn.[11]

    He has much other advice to give, some of it racy, some of it stodgy. Women are his great concern. One senses that he is chaste and reasonably happy in his marriage but thinks of women in stereotypes. He who lives by the stereotype will die by the stereotype.

    The gospel writers seem to be familiar with some of his phrases as if they were common coin. Yet they use them in a different way. Here is the Sirach version:

------

6. Sir 45:15–17   7. Sir 40:15   8. Sir 32:1   9. Sir 27:1–2
10. Sir 11:3   11. Sir 7:32, 34

Become not a glutton nor a winebibber
   with nothing in your purse. . . .[12]

When a fool hears something, he is in labor,
   like a woman giving birth to a child. . . .[13]

O death! how bitter the thought of you
   for a man at peace amid his possessions. . . .[14]

Who will trust an armed band
   that shifts from city to city?
Or a man who has no nest,
   but lodges where night overtakes him?[15]

Jesus' teaching was not only not trivial, it avoided the pragmatic. Yet it was eminently practical, an everyday ethic of the loftiest kind. Much of his speech was gnomic, meaning not only wise but puzzling. Not as obscure as the Zen *ko'an*, or riddle, his sayings could nonetheless invite a double or a triple understanding. They occurred as two- or three-line verses, interspersed with an occasional one-liner. Most often they were grouped in threes or fives, whether by him or by his followers later. Matthew's "sermon on the mount," like the other major blocks of teaching in his gospel, is a sayings collection grouped according to sense. Set in such a way as to indicate their probable original form, a handful of Jesus' sayings follow:

When a person strikes you on the right cheek,
   turn and offer him the other. . . .
Give to the man who begs from you,
   turn not your back on the borrower. . . .
When you give alms, blow no trumpet before you in
   synagogues and streets
   like actors seeking applause. . . .
When you fast, groom your hair and wash your face.

---

12. Sir 18:33   13. Sir 19:10   14. Sir 41:1   15. Sir 36:26–27

Thus no one can see you fasting but your Father
who is hidden,
And your Father who sees what is hidden will repay you. [16]

We would call this mode of discourse speaking in proverbs.
It was also speaking in poetry. The Jewish teacher of Jesus' time
chose his words carefully, speaking in phrases he hoped would
be remembered.

Everyone will be salted with fire.
Salt is good in its place,
    but if it grows tasteless how can you season it?
Keep salt in your hearts
    and you will be at peace with one another. [17]

You justify yourselves in human eyes,
    but God reads your hearts.
What humanity thinks important,
    God holds in contempt. [18]

Below is a cluster of Jesus' sayings. They are grouped by
sense in Luke's gospel. Jesus probably uttered them on a variety
of occasions:

The worldly do better than the unworldly
    when dealing with their own kind.
Make friends for yourselves through worldly goods,
    so that when they run out you will get a good reception.
If you can trust someone in small things,
    you can also trust him in greater.
If you cannot be trusted with money, easily spent,
    who will trust you with what endures?
If you cannot be trusted with another's money,
    who will give you your own? [19]

Many of Jesus' sayings echo, or have echoes in, rabbinic
literature. We should expect that. Some were the standard usage of

---

16. Mt 5:39, 42; 6:2, 17–18   17. Mk 9:49–50   18. Lk 16:15   19. Lk 16:8–12

the time. Others were placed where they were in the gospels as a commentary on his stories. At times they do not fit especially well.

The collection of five sayings immediately above seems to be such a case. Luke has reported a tale of Jesus about a crooked manager his employer admires grudgingly, even as he fires him. Having told the story, Luke tries five keys to the lock.

The first one, at least, fits in the lock. The second one turns it a little, the next three do not even do that. The door holds fast. The power of Jesus' story remains, resisting forever all certainty of interpretation.

5

The
Saint Who
Made Whole

PIETY DOES NOT HAVE A VERY GOOD NAME THESE DAYS, AND
there are reasons. It has a tendency to verbalize, often in a special
vocabulary that is more successful in including people out than in.
Piety has consistently been censorious, "holier than thou." Worst
of all, perhaps, it is associated in the popular mind with mere for-
malism: dressing, speaking, acting in certain ways calculated to
separate the pious from the nonpious.

In ancient Rome where there were no Christians and
relatively few Jews, the adjective *pius* had a no-nonsense sort of
ring to it. It was used to describe someone who was decent to his
parents, faithful to his wife, respectful toward the Roman state,
and worshipful of its goddesses and gods. The phrase "a pious slob"
is unthinkable in Latin. The adjective had too much connotation of
vigor and having-its-wits-about-it for that. In ancient Rome you
could be pious or a slob but you could not be both.

The word *hasid* in Hebrew is related to the noun *hesed* which is often translated "loving kindness." The pious are those who care greatly about life under the covenant, especially as it is expressed by fidelity to the law of Moses lived in love. The one thing certain about the *hasidim* in every age is that they are not ordinary, run-of-the-mill types. They try to depart from the conventional standard in the direction of greater, fuller Jewish existence.

There is a class of holy men reported on in the rabbinic literature who are called the "first *hasidim*." We do not know when they lived but we do possess something of their spirit. They were extremely careful about human relations and would rise above the requirements of the law to help anyone in need. They feared sin and took pains not to scandalize anyone with a tender conscience. They spent long hours in prayer, taking as much as an hour before they began to direct their hearts to God.

Since all of rabbinic writing bears the stamp of the group that came to prevail in Judaism, we are told (in its spirit) that these first *hasidim* refrained from doing anything on a weekday that could ultimately desecrate the Sabbath. This sensitivity regarding the fulfilling of various commandments may be anachronistic as a description of the earliest hasids, but some of the things reported of them are unaffected by time. For example, certain of them would bury thorns and glass deep in their fields, placing them three handbreadths down so that the plow would not displace them and thus cause people to stumble over them. That is thoughtfulness — piety — of the highest order.

Similar to these earliest holy men and not clearly distinct from them are the "*hasidim* and men of deeds." Not only did these do good deeds but the deeds they did were accompanied by miracle-working power. The little we know of this group pictures them as celebrative, singing and dancing at festivals with torches in their hands like David at the return of the ark, or like the earlier bands of "sons of the prophets." The man Honi we mentioned in Chapter 1 and his grandsons Abba Hilkiah and Hanan ha-Nehba were among these "men of deeds." So was Hanina ben Dosa, who was evidently the last of them. The deeds in question seem to be more than ordinary pious acts. They were miraculous happenings in response to the boundless faith in God's power that these saints had. Their teaching was not by words but by the courage and faith of their example.

Ḥanina ben Dosa once told his daughter to put vinegar in the lamp when the oil ran out, since, "He who commanded oil to burn will also command vinegar to burn."[1] He was bitten once by a poisonous lizard, which died. Ḥanina brought it on his shoulder to the house of study and said to those assembled: "See, my sons, it is not the lizard that kills, but sin."[2]

Not even the life of the wonderworker is free of tension, for these men of deeds seem to have been in conflict with the teachers of the path of the Torah. We know about this from passages just before and after the two we have cited from two different tractates. Ḥanina is on record as the author of a saying that seems to throw down the gauntlet: "He whose actions exceed his wisdom, his wisdom shall endure; but he whose wisdom exceeds his actions, his wisdom shall not endure."[3]

"Wisdom" is something special here. It is not just being wise—in itself no little accomplishment—but having the social status of a *ḥakam*, a sage, as well. The saying is a clear challenge by the unlearned to those who are learned. It holds action to be higher than study.

Evidently this generation of men of action was in the older, prophetic mold. The rabbinic exposition of Genesis 2:5 ("And there was not a man to till the ground") indicates as much: "There was no man to cultivate people's allegiance to God such as Elijah and Ḥoni ha-Me'aggel (The Circle-Maker)."[4] This coupling of the ancient prophet, who brought down rain from the God of Israel on Carmel, with a modern figure also hailed as a rainmaker is significant. It means that before Jews were brought to loyalty to God by the study of the Torah, the way of the rabbis, they were led by deeds of power. This is to go back beyond Amos and Hosea, Jeremiah and Isaiah, to those prophets of power, Elijah and Elisha, of whom no books or writings are reported. It is a religious primitivism based on the holy man's direct contact with God.

This is the oldest kind of human power in a setting of the divine. In a Jewish context, the persons who exercise this power are by no means disinterested in the traditions of a people. At the same time, they do not require the intermediary function of special learning with regard to those traditions. Elijah and Elisha were men of

1. *Ta'anith* 25a   2. *Berakoth* 33a   3. *Sayings of the Fathers* III, 10
4. *Genesis Rabbah* 7

the covenant, but they were primarily agents of divine power. They presumably knew the law of Moses, yet this is nowhere said of them. Written scriptures and oral traditions on the meaning of the scriptures were much later developments. The ancient prophet-wonderworkers made no appeal to a corpus of laws.

Jesus seems to have been a religious primitivist in that sense. He was not unintelligent; certainly he was not uninterested in the law. But he did not argue the case for God's dominion over his fellow-Jews exclusively in terms of the law. He was not a man of texts or authoritative interpretations of texts. In the vocabulary of the times, he was not a sage. That is what we must understand when the challenge is thrown him: "How did this man get his education when he had no teacher?"[5] He knew letters in the sense that he was literate, but he was not schooled under a rabbinic master. Much later usage worked out a distinction between a disciple (talmid) and a teacher, a rab or rabbi. The former was free to speak only on whatever he was studying currently, while the latter could range widely through all the decisions that had ever been made on the Torah. Jesus' apparent limitation was that he had never progressed as far as stage one.

This does not mean that he never made an appeal to the written law. Here are two samples of his familiarity with the text: "As to the raising of the dead, have you not read in the book of Moses how God told him, in the passage about the burning bush, 'I am the God of Abraham, the God of Isaac, the God of Jacob' ?"[6] Or again: "Have you not read in the law how the priests on temple duty can break the sabbath rest without incurring guilt?"[7]

In a dispute over the reasons that justified divorce, Jesus can be presumed to know the passage in Deuteronomy at the beginning of Chapter 24 on which the disciples of Hillel and Shammai differed. Instead of quoting what various teachers had to say on the meaning of the passage—the accepted technique—he took the argument to higher ground:

Have you not read that at the beginning the Creator made them male and female and declared, "For this reason a man

---

5. Jn 7:15   6. Mk 12:26   7. Mt 12:5

shall leave his father and mother and cling to his wife, and the two shall become as one"?[8]

The technique of quoting scripture against scripture was entirely acceptable in Jesus' day. His challengers among the learned would have noted it with approval. He is never once reported as quoting the oral law, however, the decisions of the "ancients," and this silence spoke much louder.

Did he know the variety of opinions that went to make up this oral law? He would not have been expert in them, assuming he was busy at his woodworking trade throughout his young adult years. He would, however, have been exposed to them through daily conversations and ordinary synagogue attendance. There is some dispute among the scholars of today as to whether this layman's school existed yet in Galilee in Jesus' day, but it probably did. What could not have gone unnoticed was his total disregard in later life for half the wisdom that was traded there. As has been said, he never quoted the men of the preceding century on ways to live out the precepts that changing times had rendered outmoded.

If Jesus' way of citing the law, and even more his failure to appeal to his immediate intellectual forebears, were noted by his contemporaries, his activity as a "man of deeds" could not go unnoticed. The deeds did not include rainmaking, Elijah's outstanding marvel. Its opposite, the stilling of a storm, is the only such miracle recorded of him.[9] But he did engage in a variety of healings. None of these was connected with Hanina's poisonous reptile (as was the one related in the Acts of the Apostles of Paul at Malta).[10] Instead, there was a variety of restorations of withered limbs, lost sight, and mute speech. He usually accomplished these with a word, sometimes at a distance.

Thus, to a man whose hand was shriveled up, he proposed: " 'Stand up here in front!. . . .' Then he said to the man, 'Stretch out your hand.' The man did so and his hand was perfectly restored."[11]

Jesus asked a blind man once: " 'What do you want me to do for you?' 'Rabboni,' the blind man said, 'I wish to see.' Jesus said in

---

8. Mt 19:4–5   9. Cf. Mk 4:35–41   10. Cf. Acts 28:3–6   11. Mk 3:5

reply, 'Be on your way. Your faith has healed you.' "[12]

This trust in his power to heal is praised by Jesus more than once. ("Daughter, it is your faith that has cured you.")[13] He seems to single out trust, not as a necessary condition of his miraculous activity, but as the state of heart best calculated to ensure it.

At times the cure is achieved while the sufferer is far removed from Jesus, as happened in the case of a centurion's slave: " 'Go home. It shall be done because you trust.' That very moment the boy got better."[14]

A whole series of cures is reported in which there is some bodily contact with Jesus. This was a standard detail in healing practices in the ancient world. Of a man afflicted with a scabrous disease it is told: "Moved with pity, Jesus stretched out his hand, touched him and said: 'I do will it. Be cured.' "[15] And regarding a child thought to be dead: "Taking her hand he said to her, *Talitha, koum,*' which means, 'Little girl, get up.' "[16]

The physical contact thought by many of the time to be essential for a cure was not always voluntary on Jesus' part. There is a story told of a woman hemorrhaging—menstrually, one supposes—over a period of a dozen years:

"If I only touch his clothing," she thought, "I shall get well." Immediately her flow of blood dried up and the feeling that she was cured of her affliction ran through her whole body.[17]

Mark describes Jesus as none too pleased with this surreptitious drain on his power, but that may be for narrative purposes. He asks, almost angrily, "Who touched my clothing?" but when faced with the culprit he sends her off with the standard word of departure: " *Shalom* [Go in peace], and be free of this illness.' "[18]

Like healers generally, Jesus healed through symbolic action. Once again, crying "magic" would only betray our ignorance of the Jewish world of that time: "He put his fingers into the man's ears and, spitting, touched his tongue."[19]

---

12. Mk 10:51–52   13. Mk 5:34   14. Mt 8:13; see Mk 7:30
15. Mk 1:41   16. Mk 5:41   17. Mk 5:28–29   18. Mk 5:34
19. Mk 7:33

In a later Christian writing Peter will heal with his shadow[20] and Paul through the medium of handkerchiefs and cloths.[21] None of this should be dismissed scornfully as magic. We must be as sympathetic to the folkways of ancient times as of the modern West Indies and Africa. The exercise of power without symbolism is universally unthinkable.

> Wherever he put in an appearance, in villages, in towns, or at the crossroads, they laid the sick in the market places and begged him to let them touch but the tassel of his cloak. All who touched him got well.[22]

Yet Jesus, who had the characteristics of a *hasid* who was a man of deeds, taught in words as well. This tended to confuse people. He taught differently from the way the teachers taught. The common people heard him willingly, but some of the teachers grew angry. That is only to be expected. The protection of one's image, one's role, is a universal phenomenon. Offending against traditional role-behavior is the one unforgivable sin.

---

20. Acts 5:15   21. Acts 19:12   22. Mk 6:56

6

The
Mystic

THE WORDS "MYSTIC" AND "MYSTICAL" ARE USED IN MANY contexts these days, frequently inexactly. Foggy, dreamy, and woolly-headed are a few meanings that come to mind. Irrational, intuitive, and apophatic are another such trio. All solid attempts at a definition of the term "mysticism" end by speaking of a union of the individual with, or possession by, the ultimate, whether this ultimate is conceived personally or impersonally. Some say that mystics in the theist and the nontheist tradition have all major matters in common, that their differing concepts of God and the All are of no consequence. Others say it makes an immense difference. Some who are predominantly rational in their approach to life deplore mysticism. They see in it the polar opposite of all that religion means to them and should mean to anyone. Others committed to reason welcome it as another way to achieve the good they seek, some even calling it a higher way than their own.

The mystical state is widely conceded to be the result of an immediate experience of God or the One. Trances, visions, voices, the death of the senses and the passions are not required for this experience, even though any or all may be had by an individual. The main question undoubtedly is: Is the loss of personal identity through integration with the Other or with the larger Self a requisite for mystical union? If this complete union, this becoming the other, were a necessity, mysticism would be unthinkable for anyone committed to God as that other. This has led to the conclusion that the bulk of Jewish and Islamic thinkers has reached on the inadmissibility of mysticism. The semi-official position adopted by both traditions—so expressed here because no official position is possible in either—has not hampered the existence of a vigorous mystical tradition in Judaism and Islam.

In defense of the sober expositors of the Bible and Talmud, the Qur'ān and Hadīth, who find all wisdom in those sources, it should be said immediately that they are resisting the arcane, the gnostic, the claim to bypass divinely inspired media. They are not setting a limit to God's action.

Probably because of its roots in pre-rabbinic Judaism and its congeniality with Platonism, Christianity has never declared mystical states out of bounds. The mystics often had it hard in Christian circles, especially when they failed to conform to prevailing rational patterns. But tolerance of the mystics has always been fairly lively. Rome and the Eastern churches have canonized certain mystics as saints and tended to honor rather than dishonor the rest. The Russian church has probably been the Christian mystic's best home. The Protestant reform was initially harsh on its saints, suspecting any veneration but that directed to Father, Son, and Spirit. Yet some great mystics have emerged from Protestantism, particularly the Free Church tradition that underscored the action of the Spirit.

Part of Christianity's openness to the notion of mystical union has been the development by its Greek Fathers of the idea of the divinization of the individual. This was never thought to be an apotheosis in the strict sense, the creature's "becoming God." It always meant the retention of creaturehood and proneness to sin, but at the same time a seizure by the deity of whoever would admit the activity of godhead fully into the self. This holy obsession results in no loss of selfhood, even though at times a perfect self-awareness may be forfeited. God remains God and the creature a creature, whether in the mysticism of Christian, Muslim, or Jew. The line may become wavy but it never disappears.

In Asian thought and the parts of the world influenced by it, the line has to disappear. This is an imperative not simply for mystics but for all. There, the forfeiting of consciousness that brings in its train a yielding to higher consciousness is a universal call. Many in their poverty or pain, their luxury or lust, resist it, but in the measure they do they pay the price. *Samsāra*, the endless wheel of existence, is the penalty for failure to become one with the One. The mystic in the East is not an especially gifted person nor a model for others. The mystic, like the rest of us, is an enfleshed captive who fulfills human destiny because he or she, unlike the rest of us, breaks out of the prison of individuality.

We might find it attractive to hail Jesus as a mystic because the notion is currently popular. We might wish to identify him with the Far East because the Near East's intransigent theism seems to be losing ground in the West. That would be to manipulate him cheaply for some short-term purpose. The effort founders, moreover, on what we know of him from the sources. He was irrevocably committed to Israel's God. He conceived this God not only as personal, but as deeply interested in the fate of individuals. The mystical reality that can be attributed to him is twofold: Jesus did not hold intermediaries—the Torah, learning, formal worship, religious signs—to be necessary in the search for union with God; moreover, he was constantly in a state of prayer.

This mystical reality of the man of Nazareth must be understood for what it was not, as much as for what it was. Nowhere does he repudiate Jewish peoplehood. If anything, he supports it at every turn. The great signs of it never come in for criticism on his lips: covenant, circumcision, law, temple sacrifice. It is true that the popular opinion of him in official circles—something we can deduce from the gospels rather than prove—seems to have been that he never stopped making statements against the holy place and the law. Yet the statements attributed to him that we have do not clearly sustain such a charge. Neither demonstrably anti-temple nor anti-Moses, Jesus committed the major offense of not speaking about either in the familiar way. He was a traditionalist in the radical sense of that word. Like the Samaritans, he appealed to the oldest traditions. He took his case for God's demands back to God himself. The directness of his appeal seems to have been his downfall. He admitted no authority between Israel's Father and the human conscience. This setting aside of intermediate authority in favor of ultimate authority may have been his undoing.

Any sentiment in favor of Jesus' mode of interpreting the law would be out of order here. Christians have long been given to it. The way it is normally done is to set him in contrast to the "small-minded legalists" of his time. They are charged with bad faith in their inability to recognize a prophet in their midst. He is identified as the man of good faith, whose personal holiness and teaching are irrefutable by anyone of good faith. In this confrontation—and the gospel writers were the first to engage in it—the major institutions of the Judaism of the time come under fire.

The Christian does not especially care about these institutions, which are not his or hers. The Christian has no stake in them. Shortsightedly, the supposition is made that Christian institutions are in no danger. Church, sacraments, the appeal to scripture are presumed to be rocks the teaching of Jesus cannot dash against because they *are* that teaching. The result is a painful insensitivity to the Jewish establishment of Jesus' day, not to speak of our own day. There is a consequent inability to see what the problem of Jesus in his lifetime was.

Another familiar way around the difficulty posed by Jesus in his time is to claim that the power class he fell afoul of was the priestly establishment which had as its main concern temple revenues. They were Jews, but collaborationist Jews, just as anxious as the Romans to preserve political stability. The fact that there are no modern successors to the Jewish priesthood—just as the Romans are not thought of as the ancestors of Italians (despite Mussolini's best efforts)—makes the temple priesthood an easy target. Careful study of the gospel accounts of Jesus' death seems to reveal that an alliance between the representative of the empire, Pilate, and the temple priestly element brought it about. The Pharisees who figure so importantly earlier in his career, as the gospels report it, seem to have had no part in it.

But we are not speaking of the circumstances of Jesus' death here; we are speaking of his life. Why did he not make more of an impact on Jewish life so that some contemporary sources besides Josephus, who merely notes his activity, would have recorded it? No other source does. The references to him in the Talmud are late and doubtful. Recourse to a theory of suppression of the evidence will not satisfy here, although it may serve as a partial explanation.

The fact seems to be that Jesus was so out of phase with certain patterns of Jewish contemporary teaching that the age immediately after him could not find room for the novelty he comprised. Had he confined himself to wonderworking, perhaps it could have. It probably was not the way his teaching was developed by the gospel writers or their antecedents that made the difference, not even the claim that he was the messiah or in some sense divine. His mystical union with God, uncommon in Jewish piety in that age, coupled with his lack of veneration for the oral law, would have sufficed to render him unacceptable to the teachers of his time. His followers did not walk in *halakah*, the path of observance that came to be the mark of true Jews.

Take the first matter first, the way he viewed himself in relation to God. Jesus seemed to think that communing with God in separation and in silence was of the greatest importance. Again and again it is written of him: "He stayed in desert places,"[1] or: "Rising early the next morning, he went off to a lonely place in the desert; there he was absorbed in prayer."[2]

A report made to him by his friends of their special activity—and God knows he was an activist himself—brought the invitation: " 'Come by yourselves to an out-of-the-way place and rest a little.' . . . So Jesus and the apostles went off in the boat by themselves to a deserted place."[3]

It is interesting to note that this attempt at rest and reflection ended in neither. The people's need for instruction—they were "like sheep without a shepherd"—took precedence over Jesus' need for solitude. There is nothing surprising in this, since it is the teaching of Hillel and others that human need comes before any "higher" demand. The point made here is different in that the gospels speak of union with God in prayer coupled with grueling service. In Jesus, the mystic and the holy man of deeds are combined. If there was a

---

1. Mk 1:45   2. Mk 1:35   3. Mk 6:31–32

conflict between the two roles, we are not told about it. He never comments on the demands of the crowd or his weariness from their constant pressure. He prays to his Father when he can. How much he misses the opportunity to do it more often, we can only guess.

He teaches others to pray. On one occasion the prayer he proposes to his disciples is recorded. Whether he himself prayed in the spirit of the Our Father, we cannot know. We may not forget that none of his surviving sayings has as its theme his personal repentance. He regrets nothing. Yet he tells others: "When you stand to pray, forgive anyone against whom you have a grievance so that your Father in heaven may forgive you your faults."[4]

Despite the unlimited confidence he exhibited when telling others to pray that mountains be cast into the sea,[5] he did not approach his own time of testing in the same spirit—at least as Mark recounts it:

Sit down here while I pray. . . . My heart is filled with sorrow to the point of death. Remain here and stay awake. . . . *Abba* (Father), you have the power to do all things. Take this cup away from me. But let it be as you would have it, not as I.[6]

Matthew's phrase in Jesus' best-known prayer, "Thy will be done,"[7] may be borrowed from Mark's passage above; it is not found in Luke's version of the same prayer. Luke has the following form, probably closer than Matthew to what Jesus said, since Matthew seems to work at bringing things into line with contemporary rabbinic phrasing:

Father,
hallowed be your name,
your kingdom come.
Give us each day our daily bread.
Forgive us our sins
for we too forgive all who do us wrong;
and subject us not to the trial.[8]

---

4. Mk 11:25   5. See Mk 11:23–24   6. Mk 14:32, 34, 36   7. Mt 6:10
8. Lk 11:2–4

Sometimes the Jew faults the Christian for not asking for things, saying that the Christian has fallen into a pattern of simply giving glory to God in prayer. Such a practice is strange to the Jewish ear. If the objection is valid, Jesus at least does not fall under the ban. His demands upon God are specific. Examination shows that every phrase in the Lord's Prayer can be somehow related to bringing on the Jewish "age to come." Even the word translated "daily" to describe bread is deceptive in its simplicity. No one is quite sure what it means but it seems to have to do with bread for the next day—sustenance for the hoped-for final age.

Jesus was strong on having others press a generous Father for everything they needed: "Ask and you shall receive, seek and you shall find, knock and it shall be opened to you."[9] But, again, we cannot know how much of his personal prayer was in this vein. It had to be trusting, that much is clear. God gives good gifts to anyone who asks, he said; so ask.[10]

That Jesus prayed on the occasion of taking food is recorded in the gospels, but this is what any Jew would do as he broke bread to start a meal. The blessing, it is to be noted, is not invoked on the food or on those who eat but on God, and precisely for his having given the gift of food. Nowhere is the actual wording of the blessing (berakah) at meal times recorded in the gospels. Perhaps it was thought to be too well known. There is one prayer of blessing of Jesus that is recorded; it is the only one he is likely to have spoken, since John's prayers placed on Jesus' lips are more like meditations or statements of Christian faith. The prayer referred to is in standard berakah form, first blessing God for what he has done, then immediately becoming specific:

> Father, Lord of heaven and earth, to you I offer praise; for what you have hidden from the learned and the clever you have revealed to the merest children. Father, it is true. You have graciously willed it so.[11]

There follows the claim that Jesus has received a certain fullness from God. He is the transmitter of all that his hearers need to know. Jesus calls himself, in so many words, a revealer of God. But

---

9. Lk 11:9   10. See Mt 7:11   11. Mt 11:25–26

this is the function of any authentic prophet.[12] What seems to distinguish Jesus' words is the conviction that he is not only the revealer of wisdom, but somehow in his own person the wisdom of God itself. Is the claim his or that of the gospel writer? As is often the case, it is difficult to know.

It is unwise to identify the voice of God reported both at Jesus' baptism in the Jordan and at his transformation on a high mountain as clear evidence of mystical states Mark and Matthew describe the latter as a vision. Luke says it overtook Jesus while he was at prayer. They are certainly two unusual occurrences—so much alike that they seem to be, at least from the gospel writers' standpoint, confirmations of his mission. But in such matters, who can say what is and what is not a historical happening? The luminous countenance of the visionary is so common in acccounts of mystical experience that it seems niggling to refuse it to Jesus. The witnesses, for their part, were convinced on both occasions that they had seen something extraordinary.

Jesus' prayer in his last hours shows that, wonderworker or no, he did not escape the common human lot of anguish: "My heart is filled with sorrow to the point of death."[13]

Later, from the cross, a snatch of a biblical psalm is attributed to him: "My God, my God, why have you forsaken me?"[14]

His being raised from the dead has to count as one of the most exalted states reported of anyone in the history of religious writing. Much can be said of it. At the very least it has to be called a unique condition of prayer, of uninterrupted union with the divine.

---

12. See Mt 11:27   13. Mk 14:34   14. Mk 15:34

7

The
Teacher

JESUS WAS A WANDERING TEACHER AND ḤASID. HE FOLLOWED in the footsteps of another Jewish holy man, Yoḥanan ben Zeḥariah. It is hard to know the exact relation between the two. Yoḥanan (or John) was very influential in his day. His activity is described at length by the Jewish historian Josephus, who says that King Herod imprisoned him out of jealousy of his influence with the people. Both men, John and Jesus, talked to great crowds. Both concentrated their efforts on the coming role of God as king over the Jewish people. John was so connected in the popular mind with a ritual bath in the Jordan River that history remembers him as "the Baptizer."

We know quite a lot about the ritual cleansing movements that took hold in that part of the world. Those that came after John's time were often connected with his name. Some lasted until the ninth century. Baths of purification were a thoroughly Jewish practice, specified in Moses' law after perspiration or menstruation or the use of sex. Contact with the diseased and even proximity to a dead body required a ritual cleansing. So it is not at all surprising that some would get the idea of using a bath of the whole body as a daily necesssity, others as a sign of a final break with the past.

The community rule of a pious group of Jews who began to live along the shores of the Dead Sea two centuries before John, read in part:

> [A man] shall be cleansed from all his sins by the spirit of holiness uniting him to God's truth, and his wrongdoing shall be satisfied for by the spirit of uprightness and humility. When his flesh is sprinkled with purifying water and sanctified by cleansing water, it shall be made clean by the humble submission of his soul to all the precepts of God. . . . God will cleanse man of all wicked deeds with the spirit of holiness; he will pour upon him like purifying waters the spirit of truth [to cleanse him] of all that is abominable and false. . . . The members of the covenant community shall not enter the water to partake of the pure meal of the saints, for they shall not be cleansed until they turn from their wickedness; all who offend against his word are unclean.[1]

That is the way John is described as thinking and acting when he came to the fore in the late 20s of the Common Era. (Needless to say, no one reckoned the calendar that way then.) Jesus is spoken of similarly, although it is not clear how deeply he cared about this practice of the purifying bath. The gospels say that he submitted himself to it and recruited his early followers from among disciples of John who had undergone the rite. You cannot readily learn from the gospels where he stood on its importance. Jesus was all for the reality that lay behind baptism, reform of life. His disciples of the first and second generation were busy claiming that he was more important than John, so they wrote that he baptized too—or, at least, that his followers did.[2]

Did he really baptize? We shall probably never know. What came of the rite of baptism in the Christian tradition was, first of

---

1. Community Rule of Qumrān, chapters 3, 4, and 5   2. Jn 3:26; 4:1–2

all, the placing of its chief practitioner John in second place after Jesus. John was made the first saint after the master, until in post-New Testament times Jesus' mother dislodged him. The ritual bath so closely associated with him likewise entered into the life of the community that hailed Jesus as the great prophet of God. It became the door of entry, where the power of the Spirit underlay the signs.

We can only suppose that John acted as he did because the spirit of repentance and reform was in the air. The Jews had not had a prophet they accepted as one since their return from the exile in Babylon in the 500s. Haggai and Zechariah tell us what was going on in Jerusalem during the rebuilding of the temple (520-16 B.C.E.). Among the books of the "later prophets" is a brief piece of writing done after that time, an anonymous composition called *Malachi*, "my messenger." But the prophetic spirit was gone. God had not visited his people in the person of a great prophet since those fifty years of testing by the waters of Babylon. That explains in part why John was listened to so keenly. Could he be, after this long interval, a prophet? Could he be "the prophet" spoken of in Deuteronomy, in a speech attributed to Moses?

And Jesus—where did he get the impulse to start his brief and meteoric career? We are fated not to know that either. A good and prayerful home must have produced him. He would have been trained in Hebrew letters, and at puberty been looked upon as a "son of the commandment." But that explains very little. Where does any genius, any saint or reformer come from? The answer is that in every case he or she is cast in a fresh mold. Influences can be traced but they do not account for the difference. They do not explain what is new. You must say that God raises up such a one, and leave it there.

The oppression of the Romans was one possible influence on Jesus. Galilee literally bred the Zealot movement, those extremist patriots who would not accept foreign domination in a peaceful spirit. There was Judah the Galilean who mounted a revolt at the time of Quirinius' census in 6 C.E. There were Theudas in the 40s and John of Ghiskhala, modern Jish in upper Galilee, in the 60s. There were those brave men and women at Herod's foundation fortress (*massada*) who held out for three years after Jerusalem was destroyed in 70. They were Galileans or Galilee-led, all of them. Jesus must have grown up hearing the earliest of those tales, even though they influenced him to go in another direction. They would make a boy think hard about what freedom meant and about what God had in store for his people.

Another large influence would have to have been the edifying tales told of the rabbi Hillel and his colleagues Menachem (who went off to be an Essene) and Shammai.

All the evidence from Jesus' later life is that he had a very strong self-image. He does not think or act hesitantly; he knows at all times what he is about. In his home village of Nazareth he once said: "No prophet is without honor except in his native place."[3]

On the same occasion he is reported to have likened himself to Elijah and Elisha.[4] The local people asked: "Where did he get all this?"[5] They knew his mother and his sisters and brothers too well to credit him with miracles. Mark observes briefly: "They found him too much for them."[6]

The kinship circle is standard in the Middle East, as it is in most parts of the globe. The members of an extended family are always on hand to give advice. In Jesus' case, they counseled him to keep his religious zeal from letting him make a fool of himself or get into trouble. At times they summoned him out of the crowd as one might a badly behaved child.[7] Luke softens this report of Mark to make it describe their inability to get near him.[8] At other times they come to take charge of him, saying: "He is out of his mind."[9]

That verdict was at least prompted by kinship ties. A harsher judgment put him in league with the demons of hell and its prince.[10] Except for the last reaction cited, these are fairly standard responses to anyone who comes to unexpected prominence out of humble circumstances. Jesus, or a later disciple writing of the incident, handled the loving interference of family members by describing the doing of God's will or acting on his word as greater than any ties of blood.

Jesus was considerably more brusque, even fierce, at the charge of possession by an unclean spirit.[11] That accusation conveyed to him a perverse mentality, a disposition to look at the works of holiness and declare them evil. He had no time for that

---

3. Mt 13:57   4. Lk 4:25–27   5. Mk 6:2   6. Mk 6:3   7. Mk 3:31
8. Lk 8:19   9. Mk 3:21   10. Mk 3:22–23   11. Mk 3:23–30

kind of slander against God's holy spirit. Jesus had come as one stronger than Satan to bind him so that Satan's house could be plundered. No ally of the ancient adversary does a thing like that. The devil may be evil but he is no fool. He is not divided against himself. Above all, Jesus is no mutinous servant of Satan who has broken ranks. His every word and deed show him to be at war with whatever is set against God and his holiness.

Persons who identify their cause with God's can be a frightening lot. They are often authoritarian and find in this identification the perfect expression of their will to dominate. Their deep-seated inadequacy requires them to invoke the highest power-figure possible. For people such as these, to be "with God" is the only way to cope.

It would be unwise to say too quickly, "But Jesus was not like that." We have not looked at enough of the evidence yet. We should remember that megalomania has been put forward as an explanation for his conduct from earliest times: not mere delusions of grandeur but a religious exaltation that comes with long reflection upon, a total absorption with, the power of godhead. What God can do, his servant can do. The weaker and lowlier the servant, the greater the deed of God. Some have said that in this twisted humility we have an explanation of the extravagant claims of Jesus.

Did Jesus put in a term of apprenticeship in some religious community where enthusiasm and exaltation ran high? There is nothing to support the hypothesis. The Judean desert to the south and east of Jerusalem was a seedground of body-discipline and fasting used as a means to force the divine hand. Nothing Jesus said or did lends credence to a theory of his early association with such a group. He was a townsman, not a solitary. He led a simple life as he moved about teaching, with no place to lay his head.[12] He did not boast about this, merely remarked it. He never recommended his circumstances to anyone else.

As to Jesus' abstaining from food or drink—including wine, as certain Israelites like Samson did for the duration of a vow—it never comes up except at the last meal of his lifetime. The contrary, in fact, is reported of him. He ate with anybody and everybody,

12. See Mt 8:20

and evidently ate and drank well. You cannot spread the report that a man is a glutton and a drunkard if he does not enjoy his food.[13] He accepted invitations from all kinds of people: collaborationists with landowners,[14] respected religious types,[15] and one adult family in particular.[16]

A major puzzle about this teacher is how he came to be so interested in the religion of his ancestors without being drawn into it in any of the currently traditional ways. We know that Jesus was not trained in the profession of the scribes. He seems to have been a craftsman in wood, although there is an outside chance that the gospel word for "carpenter" translates an Aramaic original, meaning "teacher." In his recorded utterances he was not very close to the visionary strain of Judaism of his time. Apocalyptic interest, as it is called, was widespread. Even the rabbis, the soberest of commentators on the law, were given to speculation about how the world as they knew it would come to an end and when. The gospels report a certain amount of this kind of language in Jesus. One can scarcely call the central positions of apocalypticism, however, his overriding concern. There is even the likelihood that the gospel writers re-apocalypticized his utterances. Divine judgment was something he cared much about and even "the end of this age," but not in the terms of the book of Enoch or even the Dead Sea scrolls.

He was not legally oriented, he was not apocalyptically obsessed. His religious concern was not political, magical, or sacrificial (that is, concentrated on the temple). What kind of Jew was this who was neither learned in the law nor interested in the overthrow of all institutions, yet who cared passionately about religion? How did he come to think the way he did? It is no wonder people asked: "Where did he get all this?"[17]

To classify him is easier than to account for him. He was interested in the human conduct of the ordinary Jew. This for him was the key to the worship of God. The strange thing about Jesus was that, although the great teachers of the years just before him cared passionately about ethics, they did so in a way he did not follow them in. This is not to say that his way was better. Chris-

---

13. See Lk 7:34   14. Lk 7:34   15. Lk 7:36
16. Lk 10:38-42; Jn 11:1-2   17. Mk 6:2

tians often make such a claim, to which Jews respond that the way of the rabbis was better. That bickering is scarcely to the point. What is at issue is that as a teacher of human behavior Jesus was quite different from what was going on around him. It is as wrong for the Christian to triumph in this as for the Jew to deplore or deny it. He was a throwback to the days of the prophets, when people felt they were impelled by God to speak and therefore spoke.

Hillel (60 b.c.e.–10 c.e.) was a Babylonian-born teacher who came to Jerusalem twice, once in 40 and again after an interval in an unknown place in 30. He was fully dedicated to the Torah (more broadly, the Lord's "instruction") and a life of *hasidut*, the way of piety. About the hermit's life and sectarianism he taught: "Do not separate yourself from the community."[18] On the urgency of his mission to teach, he said: "If I am for myself only, what am I? And if not now, when?"[19] His whole concern was with human behavior put in this context of sharing: "Love your fellow human being (of whatever sort) and draw that person nearer to the Torah."[20]

The great themes to which Hillel returned again and again were care for the common person and the poor; the cultivation of learning and discipleship, even among gentile proselytes; making human community firm against the ever-present threat of power; above all, applying the Torah to life.

Hillel despised ostentation. Like a much later figure, Kierkegaard, he made a virtue out of ordinariness. He taught:

Do not appear naked among the dressed
nor dressed among the naked;
do not stand among the seated
nor sit among those who stand;
do not laugh among the weeping
nor weep among those who laugh.
The rule is: Do not deviate from custom.[21]

Yet in one matter he could not abide lack of distinction, namely, learning. He said:

---

18. *Sayings of the Fathers*, II, 5
19. *Ibid.*, I, 14   20. *Ibid.*, I, 12   21. *Tosefta Berakoth*, 2, 21

The uneducated does not know fear of sin;
the ignorant cannot be a *ḥasid*.
The timid is not apt to learn,
the impatient is not fit to teach. . . .[22]
Do not say: "When I have leisure I shall study";
you may never have leisure. . . .[23]

A good name, once acquired, is your own possession;
he who has knowledge of the Torah has life
in the age to come.[24]

One cannot conceive of a higher doctrine than Hillel's. It is a marvel of reason and understanding, especially for the plight of the poor. It always features the gentler, the milder construction. It takes its departure from the law and ends with the law.

Be of the disciples of Aaron the priest,
loving peace, pursuing peace. . . .[25]
What is hateful to you, do not do to your neighbor;
that is the whole Torah; the rest is commentary;
go, study.[26]

While he loved the Torah, Jesus for some unaccountable reason did not refer to it in terms of constant study. Like Hillel, he wanted it lived and loved. But he was not in the tradition of the scholars, the *sopherim*. He went another way.

---

22. *Sayings of the Fathers,* II, 6   23. *Ibid.,* II, 5
24. *Ibid.,* I, 13   25. *Ibid.,* I, 12   26. *Shabbat,* 31a

8

The
Age to Come

IT WOULD BE EASY TO SAY THAT JESUS DID NOT EMERGE OUT
of the Judaism of his day as a *hasid*, or saint, because the age was
looking for a *hakam*, or sage, and he did not meet the expectation.
This may have something to do with an explanation. It is much too
simple to account for all that took place, however. The authentic
heroes of Jesus' time were committed to the Torah in a way that he
was not—even though the law meant much to him. Yet it cannot be
established that a Jew such as he, in the mold of the prophets, had
no chance of surviving in the popular imagination. Had there been
no Jesus, John the Baptizer might easily have achieved the status of
a latter-day Elijah. When John's calls for repentance went un-
heeded, the failure to repent might have been credited with bringing on the sack of Jerusalem forty years later. Jesus' appearance
subsequent to John's served to promote the figure of John in one
religious community, the Christian, and obliterate it in another, the
Jewish. It left him a vestigial remnant as an anti-hero (anti-Jesus,

that is) in a third community, the baptizing sects. As was the case with Jesus and Mary, John survived with honor in still a fourth community, Islam.

More influential than any theorizing on the fate of Jesus in history is the view that he was counted out of Jewish life because of his commitment to the end of history as something to come soon. It did not come, the theory says. Hence, the Jewish faith community was right in finding an embarrassment in Jesus. This is a serious observation and deserves to be examined. The way it is generally framed is that Jesus found congenial the spirit of flight from reality and the disregard of history that were abroad in Jewish circles, namely, apocalypticism. He found it more than congenial, he and his disciples were obsessed with it. Most of his Jewish contemporaries went unbeguiled by any such attraction. Far from mistrusting the world and history, the sages sought ways to help their fellow Jews live a fully Jewish life in their time and place. If God wished to use the Romans to tell them something about their unfaithfulness to the law, so be it. God had done the same before, using the Assyrians and the Babylonians.

Josephus reports that the Pharisees believed in "fate," while the Sadducees did not. He doubtless means a providential design, using a term familiar to Greeks in their own language.

To have a firm conviction that the end would come soon was to put one's trust in deliverance from history, not salvation through history. The question is: Did Jewish apocalyptic writers teach that? Was their discourse about "the end" really concerned with the termination of life on this earth? With the end of the world?

Jesus was quite in tune with his time in speaking of an age to come in contrast with the present age. Such was the bedrock of Pharisee hope. He shared it to the full. In this connection we must not think of "the world to come" as personal immortality, Greek-style. It was not even as simple as life after death in a bodily resur-rection of the just. It was more the assurance based on hope that, since God was faithful to his word, God would bring those who lived faithfully under the law to fruition. The divine fidelity de-manded it. This age or world was obviously not the scene of perfect justice. But the LORD had vowed justice. Therefore, death would somehow be overcome and a new era be inaugurated.

A variety of speculative writings in this vein was spawned by the Maccabean revolt. The first and best known is the biblical book of Daniel. The sight of the destruction of Jewish youth by the thousands at Greek hands brought the conviction that in a new eon the Jewish dead would rise from the dust and live again. Israel's God was a God of hope. That hope, for the Pharisee, was ultimately in victory over death.

In conversation with a woman who had just lost her brother, Jesus said by way of assurance: " 'Your brother will rise again.' 'I know he will rise again,' Martha replied, 'in the resurrection on the last day.' "[1] John's gospel reports them in easy agreement over a future reality. It then emerges that Jesus has in mind something other than the hope they share. The point is, however, that they both expect some mysterious "last day" that will usher in a new age.

This eon-theology is perhaps made clearer in Matthew when, making the account of an occurrence in Mark more specific, he has Jesus say:

Whoever says anything against the son of man will be forgiven, but whoever says anything against the holy spirit will not be forgiven, either in this age or in the age to come.[2]

In a graphic tale about heeding Moses and the prophets—all the teachers one needs, in Jesus' view—a rich man ends in torment in the abode of the dead, and a beggar in cool consolation in the bosom of Abraham.[3] This is not eon-thinking so much as a tale of God's immediate justice. But Jesus would not have told it unless he thought the popular imagination was conditioned for it.

His word to a fellow-victim from the cross is in the same vein: "I assure you, this day you will be with me in paradise."[4]

While these instances reflect the widespread conviction that death would be followed by just retribution at God's hands, they do not precisely reinforce the eon-theology we are tracing. Jesus' parables are much the best place to look for it. For example:

When the crop is ready [a farmer] "wields the sickle, for the time is ripe for harvest."[5]

---

1. Jn 11:23–24   2. Mt 12:32   3. See Lk 16:19–26   4. Lk 23:43
5. Mk 4:29

The mustard seed . . . once it is sown . . . springs up to become the largest of the shrubs, with branches big enough for the birds of the air to build nests in its shade.[6]

"No," he replied, "pull up the weeds and you might take the wheat along with them. Let them grow together until harvest. Then at harvest time I will order the harvesters: First collect the weeds and bundle them up to burn, then gather the wheat into my barn."[7]

In all these agricultural examples, a time lies ahead when humanity will flourish. The figure of the mustard bush is based on a parable in Ezekiel. The first and third feature the "day of the LORD" of the eighth- and seventh-century prophets, when he will come in judgment to sustain the good and punish the wicked. Other examples from Jesus' parables follow:

When [the dragnet] was full they hauled it ashore and sat down to put what was worthwhile into containers. What was useless they threw away. That is how it will be at the end of the world.[8]

With that [the tenant farmers] seized him, dragged him outside the vineyard, and killed him. What do you suppose the owner of the vineyard will do to them when he comes?[9]

When once the master of the house has risen to lock the door and you stand outside knocking and saying, "Sir, open for us," he will say in reply, "I do not know where you come from."[10]

You can find the same idea put more subtly, that is, without the imagery of force or violence, in many other of Jesus' stories. A man asks his two sons to help him work in the family vineyard. One says he will, but does not. The other says he will not, but does. Jesus asks: "Which of the two did what the father wanted?"[11]

This hint of a twofold outcome, one for those responsive to his preaching and another for the resistant, underlies many of Jesus'

---

6. Mk 4:31–32   7. Mt 13:29–30   8. Mt 13:48–49
9. Mt 21:39–40   10. Lk 13:25   11. See Mt 21:28–31

stories. The theme common to most is the working out of justice, irresistibly and beyond appeal, in the future. Often in Jesus' brief vignettes nature takes its time, by which we are to understand that God takes his time. The seed grows, the dough rises, the fig tree buds, all in due season. In stories of human activity the house built on rock lasts, the judge vindicates the widow, the employer pays everyone at the same rate. It all works out somehow. Justice, often mystifying justice, is done—later. Tolstoi puts the main point of Jesus' stories when he says, "God sees the truth, but waits."

What is destined to come is God's reign, whether humanity expects it or not, prepares for it or not. The notion of God's kingly rule was an old one in Israel, so much so that the people were convinced that they had no king but him. Neither Saul nor David nor Solomon, neither Judahites or Ephraimites, Hasmoneans or Herodians were kings in the eyes of the Jews as other nations had kings. The LORD was king and he alone.

References to this dominion of God over the Jewish heart are found everywhere: in the Bible, in the literature of apocalyptic eschatology (a vision of "the last days") that came after it, in the writings of the rabbis, in the writings of the Christians. The one matter that is a constant is God's reign. The word "kingdom" does not convey the idea very well, nor does "kingship." The reality is far too active and relational for that. It is the subduing in freedom of that most restless of creatures, the human heart. The dream that recurs in every stage of Jewish life envisions the hearts of a whole people obediently submissive to its LORD.

Whereas this ideal reign or rule is encountered at every turn, only within a limited period does the expectation occur that God will break in on his people forcibly and exact dominion. His own people will submit willingly, his enemies (*their* enemies) cravenly. The time around 175 B.C.E. is the starting point of such writings, 135 C.E. the terminus. The first of those dates marked a revolutionary spirit that led to victory over the Seleucid dynasty of Greeks, the second, a political defeat by Rome that proved final for the Jews. In between, a visionary literature proliferated that saw a cataclysmic end to the world as we know it: the sun darkened, stars falling from the skies, people withering with fear. In a final conflict, God and the sons of light would take the measure of all the forces that dwelt in darkness. The heavens and the earth would pass away. There would succeed a millennium and many millennia of prosperity and peace.

This kind of thinking is reflected in a snatch from one of the *Hymns* of the community of Qumrân along the shores of the Dead Sea:

> The floods of Belial shall go over all steep
> banks like a devouring fire
> Consuming every tree, green and barren, in
> their channels.
> It shall sweep with burning flames until all
> who drink of them are no more.
> It shall consume the foundations of the earth
> and the expanse of dry land.
> The foundations of the mountains shall blaze
> and the roots of flint become streams of pitch.
> It shall devour down to the deep Abyss.[12]

We should note immediately that this is the only passage in the scrolls of a supposedly apocalyptic community that *may* speak of the end of the world. Close inspection of all the literature of the period shows that "the end" is more a time of crisis than a definite end. Very clearly conveyed by the colorful language are notions such as cataclysm, conflict, and purgation—but always with the underlying theme of a new start. Apocalyptic eschatology was a literature of hope, not of destruction. The "apocalypse" spoken of was the disclosure of the prophetic vision of the LORD's supreme rule, usually of a hidden or in-group kind. How he will deal with his people in the future, how he will rearrange the cosmos, is all there. But the language is figurative to the point of inscrutability.

Many, in fact most, have interpreted this colorful writing as the reflection of a pessimistic view of reality that grew out of the bleak prospects of Judaism after the exile. The theory is that, discouraged with life on the earth, the people's poets held out to them a life under new heavens on a new earth. But for this to be true, the poetic imagery must be taken literally, which is death to the intent

---

12. Column III, 29–33

of a poet. The language must also have a deep pessimism as its theme, whereas, in fact, it stresses new beginnings.

The apocalyptists spun their webs of fancy on a loom of hope. They employed myth to help their readers live life and transcend death. If they proclaimed an end, it was in the interests of a fresh start. The new humanity sketched out had, to be sure, elements of the angelic and the heavenly. But how else could the reality of the new age be conveyed, with its setting aside of all the distressing limitations of the present one?

Jesus spoke at times in the poetic language that was his inheritance from Daniel, Zechariah, and the non-biblical apocalypses that preceded him.

The heavens and the earth will pass away, but my words will not pass away.[13]

During that period, after trials of every sort, the sun will be darkened, the moon will not shed its light, stars will fall from the heavens, and the heavenly hosts will be shaken. Then the son of man will be seen coming in great glory. I assure you, this generation will not pass away until all these things take place.[14]

Matthew even appears to have accommodated a judgment-scene poem, in which YHWH had been the judge, to Jesus:

When the son of man comes in his glory, escorted by all the angels of heaven, he will sit upon his royal throne and all the nations will be assembled before him. Then he will separate them into two groups as a shepherd separates sheep and goats.[15]

From utterances like these attributed to Jesus it has been assumed that he was apocalyptic, that is to say, nonrealistic, in his outlook. It is also widely assumed that he expected the end of the world to come soon. One needs to be ignorant of the kind of Hebrew speech attributed to him to make a claim like that with certainty. He expected judgment to come in the future. He expected it

---

13. Lk 21:33   14. Mk 13:24–26, 30   15. Mt 25:31–32

to come suddenly. He was certain it would come. "Soon" is the apocalyptic word for this expectation, but it lacks the ordinary connotations of time.

Jesus had an urgency of tone about the reality of the impending crisis that few in his time who were interested in the everyday choices of Jewish life shared. He was too deeply interested in continuing patterns of human conduct to be accused of thinking that things were, in Edwin Albee's title, "All Over."

He preached, rather, a new beginning, which his own generation was going to witness.

He predicted the impending end of "this age."

For those who came to believe in him, under God he brought it about.

9

The
Reluctant
Messiah

WHO DID JESUS THINK HE WAS? A BETTER WAY TO PUT THE question is: What did he think his role was? The data the gospels provide show from his actions that he knew exactly who he was and what he had come to do. The questions as we have put them do not find an immediate answer. The reason is evident. The men who wrote the gospels made it so clear who *they* thought he was that they left little room for Jesus' own estimate of himself. We have to conclude to a self-image of Jesus from those deeds and words reported of him that seem to be least interpreted by the gospel writers. It is by no means easy to know which these are. In this question, it is better to offend by claiming to know too little than too much. This is true if only because those who wrote about him were already committed believers in him.

Jesus thought he was a son of Abraham who had the full liberty of all the children of the promise. The terms of the covenant with Israel's God bound him, but nothing else. Even then, he sat lightly to the saddle of those demands. It is hard for us to get hold of the total freedom he thought he had, especially if we have been raised in the milieu of a Jewish establishment or a Christian establishment or a secular establishment set against the other two. The evidence is that he considered himself absolutely free and self-determined. He was inhibited by no authority or opinion. Parenthetically (and quite seriously), this may be why it later occurred to others to attribute divinity to him. "In the kingdom of the blind the one-eyed man is king." It would be a tragic commentary on our race if someone who seemed completely free in his humanity were to be hailed for it as more than a man. There comes to mind irreverently the comment of the Pullman porter who said that the average tip on his run was five dollars but there hadn't been many come up to the average lately.

There are many who are self-determined, self-motivated, uninfluenced by anyone—or so it seems. They exist in distressing numbers. Yet Jesus spoke and acted like someone in a different mold. His conduct was totally free within limits he himself knew. His description of this limit factor was the will of God, or as he put it, the will of "the Father." Jesus was beholden to no human opinion. He never quoted his parents, learned rabbis, or any authority figure. This was remarkable in one so young—he can only have been thirty-five or so at his death—especially in the light of the mental maturity that accompanied this self-sufficiency. The non-dependent are usually brash. Jesus was not brash.

He must have been reared in a household that breathed freedom. Reflecting much on what it meant to be a human being, to be a son of God, to be a Jew, was surely the absorption of the years we know nothing about.

The easiest question raised in connection with Jesus' self-awareness is: Did he think he was Israel's messiah? The answer seems to be an unequivocal no. It is wisest to view him on his own terms, not the terms of those who harbored the messiah notion. He spoke with great assurance in his attempts to disclose God's will to others. For this he must be called a man of prophetic insight. What is said of Israel's prophets has to be said of him—"prophet" understood not as a foreteller or seer but as someone who has been given a tongue and has to speak. The prophets whose names are attached to written books, even as Moses and Elijah before them, commented on the events of their times as they saw them. They gave unsolicited advice. They were convinced they knew the meaning of what was going on around them. They could not remain silent.

Jesus was strangely nonpolitical as prophets of Israel go. He was intensely interested in the corporate behavior of his people but not in its relation to the Roman republic or Greek civilization. Each of the latter in its way threatened to engulf Israel. If he was apprehensive about them, he did not say. He seemed interested only in situating the Jewish people before God. You might call his teaching either a timeless conservatism or an up-to-date radicalism. His immediate goal was the ethical one of individual right-doing. Yet he accepted the title of prophet—a title with social overtones—and may even have used it of himself.[1]

The title "messiah" was much bandied about in Jesus' time, a word of small occurrence in the Bible and then chiefly in the psalms to designate a king. The book of Isaiah at 45:1 called Cyrus of Persia "messiah" because God had singled him out to release the Jews from captivity. The gospel writers make clear in a great number of ways that they think Jesus was the king-messiah. They have him approving his friend Simon for the insight that recognizes him to be such.[2] Mark has Jesus applying the title "Christ" (messiah)[3] to himself and acknowledging to the high priest the night before he suffers that he is indeed that.[4] John shows him doing the same with a Samaritan woman earlier in his career.[5]

Yet if you look more carefully, you see that every time the title is used it is in the context of a statement of someone else's faith in him, not his view of himself. The demons he exorcises call him "son of God" rather freely, and he does not argue the point.[6] But when, more rationally, people do it, he is totally ill at ease with the attribution of kingship. He dismisses the title with declarations that he needs to suffer and die, a notion simply not connected with that of a king—victorious by definition in the popular mind.[7]

---

1. See Mt 10:41; 13:57   2. See Mt 16:17; but compare the earlier Mk 8:29–30
3. See Mk 9:41   4. See Mk 14:61–62   5. See Jn 4:26
6. See Mk 1:24; 3:11; 5:7   7. See Mk 8:30–31

Even the argument put on Jesus' lips by Mark—whether it was Mark who framed it or Jesus himself—is a way of saying that the psalm is praising a mysterious personage for something other than Davidic kingship:

> How can the scribes claim, "The messiah is David's son"? David himself inspired by the holy spirit said, "The LORD said to my lord: Sit at my right hand until I make your enemies your footstool."[8]

Whatever this may mean, it is a challenge to the conventional wisdom about kingship.

The fourth gospel contains a complex dialogue of Jesus with Pilate, giving reasons why Jesus' kingship, if there were any such thing, was not a matter of ordinary political rule.[9] Earlier, the same gospel portrayed Jesus as fleeing "to the mountain alone" when it seemed that by popular enthusiasm "they would come and carry him off to make him king."[10] He himself does not seem to have a very good opinion of the way sovereigns rule: "Earthly kings lord it over their people. Those who exercise authority over them are called their 'benefactors.' It cannot be that way with you."[11]

All of this together makes it a puzzle why his followers, after his death, should have visited on him a title he seemed totally ill at ease with. This, in turn, is part of a larger question: Were the scribes as absorbed with the question of a messiah as son of David as the exchange involving the quotation, "The LORD said to my lord," seems to indicate?

In Jesus' day there were numerous claimants to kingship in Israel, and numerous military uprisings—all of them aborted—which Josephus reports upon. This evidence, plus a fragment of Luke in his history of the early Christians,[12] goes well with the indications in the gospels that the populace was looking for some kingly or military deliverance. The scribes were probably responsible for the opinion that God would achieve deliverance for his people through a descendant of David.

---

8. Mk 12:35-36   9. See Jn 18:36-37   10. Jn 6:15
11. Lk 22:25-26   12. See Acts 5:35-37

A number of popular leaders, it is true, had no such Davidic credentials, but then neither did the house of Herod. It became a convention of the period to devise Davidic ancestry for hoped-for great ones. Jesus was no exception, as the accounts of the circumstances of his birth in Matthew and Luke show. But as to any single, widespread theological expectation of a figure to be known as "the messiah," that was not a demonstrable Jewish reality from Jewish sources in the age that immediately preceded Jesus. The "days of the messiah," yes, but not a distinct individual. People were much more alert to the prophet Deuteronomy has Moses promise,[13] or to Elijah who would usher in the last age.[14] They seem to have come to expect a messiah-figure only shortly before Jesus' lifetime, probably prompted by the Galilean liberation movement. This confusion of roles would explain the questions raised about Jesus in several places in the gospels. The new and the older traditions are testified to, side by side, in John:

> Some . . . began to say, "This must be the prophet." Others were claiming, "He is the messiah." But an objection was raised: "Surely the messiah is not to come from Galilee? Does not scripture say that the messiah, being of David's family, is to come from Bethlehem?" ". . . Do not tell us you are a Galilean too," they taunted him. "Look it up. You will not find the prophet coming from Galilee."[15]

The newer expectation is reflected in the questions raised about the identity of the Baptizer: "The people were full of hope, wondering in their hearts whether John might be the messiah."[16] Or about Jesus: "Play the prophet for us, messiah! Who struck you?"[17]

By the time Matthew wrote his gospel, the search for such a figure had already reached a crescendo:

> If anyone tells you at that time, "Look, the messiah is here," or "He is there," do not believe it. False messiahs and false prophets will appear, performing signs and wonders. . . .[18]

---

13. See Dt 18:15; John 1:25; Acts 3:22
14. See Jn 1:21, 25; Mt 11:14; 17:11–12; Lk 1:17   15. Jn 7:40–42, 52
16. Lk 3:15   17. Mt 26:68   18. Mt 24:23–24

The picture drawn by all these references taken together is one of a widespread popular search for an anointed king who would prove to be a liberator. Jesus neither covets the role nor claims it on "spiritual" terms. Yet his followers quite clearly thought of him under that title. Here are two passages reflecting that later concern:

[The Judeans] . . . had agreed . . . that anyone who acknowledged Jesus as the messiah would be put out of the synagogue.[19]

Anyone who gives you a drink of water because you belong to the messiah will not, I assure you, go without his reward.[20]

In both of the above places the Semitic word *mashiah* has been translated into its Greek equivalent, *christos*. Only John keeps a transliterated version, *messias*, and he does this twice.[21] Clearly what has happened is that after Jesus' death there has been bestowed on him a role and a title that in his lifetime he strongly resisted.[22] He is also being preached as the Deuteronomic prophet[23] and God's servant.[24] Yet the title *christos* comes to prevail—even in Greek, to become part of Jesus' name.[25] Having been acknowledged "Jesus the Christ," he becomes "Jesus Christ."

What can account for this reversal that he himself would have found so unwelcome?

We can only conclude that Jewish hopes for freedom reached such a pitch between the years 30 and 50 that Jesus' followers decided that presenting him as the long-awaited deliverer was the best way to make their point as to who he was in the life of the Jewish people.

---

19. Jn 9:22   20. Mk 9:41   21. Jn 1:41; 4:25
22. See Acts 2:31-32, 36; 5:42   23. See Acts 2:30; 3:22
24. See Acts 3:13, 26   25. See Acts 2:38

10

The
Jesus
Jesus Recognized

THE LAST CHAPTER ENDED BY ANSWERING A DIFFERENT
question than it opened with. It described a title that Jesus was not
interested in, "messiah," and hinted only briefly at one he was at
ease with, "prophet."[1] He claimed the latter more by action than by
spoken word.

Before we get into a discussion of the title "prophet," we
ought to deal with an important popular confusion. Jews and
Christians alike tend to have a formula that goes: "For centuries the
Jewish people have expected a messiah. The main difference between Jews and Christians is that Christians believe that Jesus is the
messiah, whereas Jews still wait for his coming." There is a certain
validity to those statements from the vantage-point of the present,

---

1. See Mt 21:46; Jn 6:14

but in Jesus' day the first part was surely wrong and the second became true only after his lifetime. What had been expected since the return from the exile was a restoration of the house of David. This was thought to be God's surest way to prove his faithfulness. It was not the only way, however. When Mattathiah of Modein, a priest (hence not Davidic) and the father of five sons, threw off Greek rule in a bold uprising, no one faulted the providential plan. When one of the sons began a dynasty known as the Hasmoneans (the ancestral family name, after Hashmon, a priest), no one complained that he was of the tribe of Levi, not Judah.

With the petering out of this royal family and its defeat by the Romans in 63 B.C.E., the Davidic dream was once more revived. But the dream of a final age was gaining currency along with the hope of restoration of the royal line. It is not true to say that the two came together. Nothing was ever quite that neat in Jewish life. It would be better to say that, while the dream of a final age was ascendant in Jesus' day, some placed a Davidic king in the center of that age and some did not. Political turbulence was the reality of the present. Lasting peace was the hope of the future.

The Christian movement modified the Jewish dream in one direction; rabbinic Judaism modified it in another. The followers of Jesus proposed him in the role of messiah and worked out a genealogy (actually two) and a set of proofs from the Bible in support of their acknowledgment of him. A change in the popular conception was built into the very fact of belief in Jesus. The notion, amorphous at best, was fixed in a new way by the naming of this non-warrior, non-king, nonviolent *hasid* to the role. Judaism, meanwhile, having gone largely untouched by the Christian movement, developed its own variety of images to describe the messianic era.

In the Christian case a character sought a setting; in the Jewish case a setting sought a character. With the passage of time the twin symbolism of "the days of messiah" and "the messiah" became mutually influential, as Jew and Christian learned the threat that each posed for the other. The two symbol-systems took on certain details from one another. They did not fuse, but they did become both closer and farther apart.

Meanwhile, it is folly for Christians to fault Jews or Jews Christians for departure from a fixed biblical ideal. There was no such fixed ideal. The concept was entirely fluid in the centuries after the exile. Two groups gave it a fixity of two different kinds, at first quite independently, later by way of claim and counterclaim. When Jews say, therefore, that Jesus cannot be the messiah because universal redemption has palpably not been achieved, they are applying a standard derived from their own later, developed system of thought. When Christians ask Jews, as they began to do very early, why they do not accept Jesus as the messiah, they forget that it was they who provided their norm for messiahship in the first place by naming the man.

It is unintelligent of people who say they seek peace to press for it in terms of a division that is built into the very search.

Problems similar to those attending the title "messiah" (and its cognate, "son of David") accompany all attempts to explore the designations in the gospels of Jesus as "lord" and "son of God" and "son of man." The four writers had something honorific in mind in the case of each title. That much is clear. More than that, they were proposing for Jesus in all three cases a transcendent, not to say a heavenly, reference. The basic problem is: Did Jesus ever speak or think of himself on any such terms?

John Henry Newman once said to Charles Kingsley in exasperation—the question at issue was the regard for truth of the Catholic clergy—"*Mean* it? I maintain I never *said* it. . . ."

The key to what Jesus meant about himself is what he said about himself and that, unfortunately, is all but impossible to know. That is because we have an extensive record of what his devotees said about him, in which they often put their own faith in him on his lips. What part of that record came from his own lips is very hard to determine.

Take a frequent designation of Jesus in the gospels, "lord." It is widely supposed that the term "lord" (*kyrios*) has a ring of divine mastery about it. There is some evidence that this word was used in the translations of the Jewish Bible in Greek (the Septuagint) not transmitted by Christians for the two names the God of Israel was known by, YHWH and *'adōn*. It also meant "master"; indeed, it is the modern Greek word for "mister." A good case can be made—and has been made—for its being a rendering in the gospels of the Aramaic title *mar*. There are indications that to designate Jesus *mar* in his lifetime would have been the ordinary, respectful way of addressing a holy man. In such case, we would then have the familiar phenomenon of change of connotation with change of language; here it would be an inclining toward the sacred or the numinous when Christians became a Greek-speaking community, because Greek divinities were called *kyrioi*, "lords," and the God of Israel, "LORD."

"Son of God" provides a similar case. In Semitic and Egyptian usage the term can mean a king, but it can also mean—as it does in the Bible—any pious Jew. This term, so redolent of divinity in a Hellenist milieu, signifies any pious man before God in a Jewish speech setting. It originated in the latter, Semitic, sense. In time it was elevated to the former, Hellenist, understanding. A paradox is that "son of God" would mean a man to the Jewish ear, while "son of man" was able to convey much more.

"Son of man" is the hardest case of all. It occurs on Jesus' lips frequently as his own self-designation and is never attributed to anyone else. Yet it falls out of later Christian usage (it occurs only once in the book of Acts at 7:56, and John has it in a different sense than the first three) almost entirely.

The question is: Did Jesus speak of himself as "the son of man"? This question is hotly debated by the learned. The better answer seems to be yes. What could he have meant by the phrase? Again, the argument is vigorous. It would seem, on balance, that the connotation of the term in the book of Daniel, where it describes in a vision a symbolic figure receiving judgment in the name of many, is not what Jesus had in mind when he used it, if he used it. That, however, was clearly the gospel writers' understanding of the "son of man." They have another use of the term, employing it to describe Jesus the innocent sufferer.

It is not easy to establish that the visionary Danielic sense or even the suffering one was Jesus' understanding of the term. A much better conclusion, deriving from Aramaic usage of the time, is that it meant "the man" in the sense of "this man." Some even hold that it was a possible way of saying, "I." The term does not, in any case, convey grandiosity, as consistent reference to oneself in the third person might to us. It was, on any reckoning, a form of emphatic speech, a way to distinguish the speaker clearly.

The above discussion, starting with the beginning of the chapter, is by no means an essay in reductionism, seeing how little need be said about Jesus, in a spirit contrary to all Christian sensibilities. It compresses shelves of writing. What it maintains is that while the awe-filled intent of the gospel writers is clear from their vocabulary about Jesus, his view of himself is not to be discovered from a variety of honorific titles he probably never used. And while the gospel writers' use of "son of man" may well have been Danielic, his own use of it cannot be proved to aspire to any such heights. Some say, he may have held that a mysterious "son of man" would judge his hearers at the judgment, in accord with the heed they paid his, Jesus', words. But even that is doubtful.

A favorite way of looking into Jesus' mental life used to be to examine carefully the narratives of his baptism in the Jordan. These, it was supposed, reflected his recently dawned consciousness that he was the messiah of Israel. But the reader is reminded of the confusions on this point spoken of in previous chapters, confusions created by the evangelists who were busy describing a descent of God's spirit on Jesus, making him superior to John.

Another, similar line of inquiry was to explore his early successes at preaching in Galilee. These culminated, it was supposed, in Simon's acknowledgment at Caesarea Philippi that he was the Christ, and in his later transformation in appearance on "a high mountain."[2] Both occasions encompassed the realization that he had to suffer and to die. This awareness, the theory ran, was an intimation of all the rebuffs he would receive at the hands of the ruling and the learned classes in Judea. From that point on, his teaching was a failure, almost in the measure it had heretofore been a success.

The chief flaw in any such scheme—a Galilean ministry followed by a Judean one, with Caesarea Philippi as the turning point—is that it supposes that Mark, who devised the basic story-flow of the gospels, was interested either in Jesus' thought processes or a chronological account of what happened to him. He was concerned with neither. His narrative groupings were on another principle. Mark's main interest was in what he and fellow believers thought of Jesus, not what Jesus thought of himself. He placed Caesarea Philippi at the midpoint of his gospel for dramatic narrative purposes, surely not for psychological.

---

2. See Mk 8:27–30; 9:2–8

Are we, then, to be thoroughly thwarted in our search for the way Jesus viewed his own person and work? The answer is: We are to be thwarted largely but not thoroughly.

We have said we have only his words to go on; of these his edited parables and proverbial sayings are the most dependable. How did his discourse betray his innermost thoughts, this man of whom some would-be captors said, "No one ever talked like that before"?[3] We have already spoken of his complete self-confidence. He entertained neither hesitation nor doubt. He did not acknowledge any weakness or sin. This, in a holy man who is not a charlatan, is unusual. He taught his hearers to judge themselves but not to judge others. He judged others but not himself. That paradox provides food for thought.

Jesus had a lively consciousness of God, whom he called Father and even *Abba*, an Aramaic term of endearment for one's father. The gospels distinguish so carefully between his use of "my Father" and, where others are concerned, "your Father" or "our Father" that the distinction may have originated with him. His was the mystic's easy and constant communion with God. The God others sought, Jesus possessed.

The evangelist John composed long soliloquies and prayers that he put on Jesus' lips. This procedure would strike us as quite unjustified if we did not have the record of Jesus' intimate orientation toward God in the first three gospels.

John reports lively debates on whether or not Jesus was a good man. Some affirmed it; others maintained he was only misleading the crowd.[4] He was accused of being in league with Beelzebul (as unedited, "abode of Baal," but by two execrable puns, "lord of dung," if the word ended in an "l," or of "flies," if it ended in a "b," Beelzebub).[5] He rejected hotly this intimation of a connection between the powers he possessed and the demons of hell, manifested in two scornful names for Canaanite deities. Still, when a man called him "good teacher," he checked him by saying: "Why do you call me good? No one is good but God."[6] One suspects that

---

3. Jn 7:46   4. See Jn 7:12   5. See Mk 3:22   6. Mk 10:17–18

the inquirer, in kneeling before Jesus, was, for Jesus' taste, too interested in his person and too little in his message.

Jesus is exclusively concerned with the coming of God's reign. He is concerned in terms of human readiness for it. Behavior is a good way to prove readiness. He never suffers doubt that the reign of God is a future reality. It will come as surely as bread rises, as grain grows, as a crop matures to be harvested. In this certainty of the future, which for Jesus is at least in its beginnings a present reality, he has a major part. He not only has a vocation to proclaim the divine rule; he has a role in bringing it on.

All the words of Jesus, in sum, come to a conviction on his part that he is not ordinary. He is empowered, gifted, touched. He must teach, he must be strengthened by God, he must suffer. He will be proved right—not by human beings but by God.

The one thing that stands out clearest in the matter of who Jesus thought he was is that he saw himself as a human instrument to achieve God's purpose. This instrumentality was a situation without limits, except for the human heritage of mortality. Jesus had to be tempted, he had to die like others. For the rest, his self-image in the gospels is so strong that it is understandable why after his death the conviction might have arisen that here was no ordinary man.

Not even the usual extraordinary man.

11

The
Jesus of
John's Gospel

ONE NEEDS TO BE WARY ABOUT THE USE ONE MAKES OF THE
gospel according to John. It contains some soliloquies that it calls
the speech of Jesus, written in their entirety by the author. They are
wonderful statements of faith about Jesus, but they should not be
thought of as his words about himself.

"I am the door," Jesus says in John's gospel. "I am the sheep-
fold, the good shepherd, the true vine. I am life. I am resurrection,
way, truth, gate. I am the living bread, the light of the world."
Briefest of all, "I am."

This mysterious mode of speech is found elsewhere in ancient literature. The goddess Isis attributes any number of names
and powers to herself. So does Hebrew wisdom, the heavenly
hokmah of the *hakamim* encountered in earlier chapters. This helps
to pinpoint an important question about John's gospel. Is it the
product of a Greek religionist who knew his Hebrew Bible, or a

Jewish sage who knew his popular Plato? The debate has raged for many decades. Those who favor the second position have the edge.

John, whoever he was, was probably a Jew trying to convince fellow Jews in some diaspora city—that is, of the Mediterranean world outside Palestine—that God's wisdom had appeared as a man. Any claim that could be made for any philosophy, for any expression of the divine *logos* (thought, world order, reason), for any pagan deity, could be made for Jesus. He was God's word made flesh, a revealer sent down from above to bring believers in him back to the realm he had come from. John's chief biblical theme is the heavenly wisdom that was with God from the beginning. He also enjoys, however, interpreting Jesus as a latter-day Moses, even a prophet-king. Jesus is a leader on a journey, a teacher, the giver of a law, the one who sustains with heavenly bread.

John possesses a number of miracle stories about Jesus like those of Matthew, Mark, and Luke. He invariably makes different use of them than they. The three healing miracles he reports are the cure of a royal official's son at Capernaum;[1] of a young man blind from birth at Jerusalem;[2] and the resuscitation from the dead of Lazarus, brother to Luke's Martha and Mary,[3] at Bethany. The only things John has overtly in common with the other three gospels are Jesus' baptism in the Jordan,[4] his multiplication of bread and fish[5] (to which is attached a story about walking on the water),[6] and the account of Jesus' last days, followed by his risen life.[7] There is an account in John of a final meal taken with his friends, but the things that Jesus says and does on that occasion are quite different from what others have to tell.[8] John also reports on Jesus' angry driving the sellers out of the temple. He situates it at the beginning of his public career, rather than at the end where the others put it.[9] And he makes it a story of the new temple of his risen body.

Many of the best-remembered stories about Jesus appear only in John. Among them are the changing of water into wine at

---

1. See Jn 4:46–54   2. See Jn 9:1–7   3. See Jn 11:1–44   4. See Jn 1:19–34
5. See Jn 6:1–13   6. See Jn 6:16–21
7. See Jn 18—21; also 12:12–15 (Mk 11:1–10); 12:1–8 (Mk 14:3–9)
8. See Jn 13:1—17:26 (Mk 14:17–26)   9. See Jn 2:13–17

the marriage feast at Cana, [10] the visit of the Pharisee Nicodemus under cover of night, [11] the exchange with Pilate about the meaning of truth, [12] and the story of doubting Thomas. [13]

Everyone interested in the teacher of Nazareth would like to know if John's stories are based on fact. When the narratives coincide with material found in the first three gospels, the problem does not arise so much. When John is on his own, however, how can he be checked on? He sometimes starts with a brief miracle story, as the others do, creates a bridge to where he wants to go, and then launches into a meditation on what Jesus means for the believer in terms of the miracle or "sign." Since his lengthy musings—with Jesus invariably the speaker—seem to be occasioned by what are in some cases historical reminiscences, there is no reason to suppose that such is not the fact with all of them. We may assume John has some fragment of narrative that he uses as a peg to hang his prose-poems on: a wedding, a pilgrimage feast, a woman at Jacob's well at midday.

How extensive the vignettes originally in John's possession were, we shall never know. All we know is what he makes of them. He proceeds by way of symbols: water as the slaker of thirst, light as the medium of eyes that see, jars of new wine as the vintage befitting celebration of Israel's marriage with God. The fourth gospel looks to the future for fulfillment, but in a unique way it finds the last age present now. "The hour is coming," John writes at 4:23, "indeed has already come. . . ." He illustrates this view of his more than once.

John does not tell any parables that are developed stories. Still, his gospel is rich in figures, words, and ideas used in a transferred sense. The better one knows the Bible, the more success one will have in reading John. Yet John never tells a tale or uses a metaphor in quite the way it appears in his sources. He is a master of allusion, a poet adept at reweaving old strands to show new designs. What many of the later Hebrew biblical authors do with earlier material, John does strikingly well. The difference is that with him everything comes up showing the face of Jesus the Christ.

---

10. See Jn 2:1–11   11. See Jn 3:1–21   12. See Jn 18:33–38
13. See Jn 20:24–29

He leaves a sour taste in the mouth for one strange reason: he consistently calls the enemies of Jesus in Jerusalem "the Jews." That is what the Greek term seems to say, although some have suggested it should be translated "the Judeans" in most instances. At times it does not seem to mean either, but rather "those Jews who did not believe in Jesus" or "Christian Jews who did not believe in him properly." The term "Israel," contrariwise, is always a high-value term for John.

The cruel paradox is that the fourth gospel is the only one where Jesus does not move about in gentile lands or show any interest in non-Jewish people, apart from Samaritans. The "Greeks" who ask Philip to see Jesus may be an exception. Some think the author is a religiously sophisticated diaspora Jew pleading and arguing with the Jews of his region to give Jesus a hearing as the Jerusalemites have not done. A few think we have in the bitter exchanges between Jesus and "the Jews" a near-transcript of the sparring of one of Jesus' defenders (the author?) with adversaries of his own place and time. Whatever the case, it is tragic that this piece of writing that has contributed so richly to the world's literature should also have contributed so heavily to the sufferings of the Jewish people. An internal religious struggle in Judaism, which is what it seems to have been, became the charter of a struggle between Jews and others.

The Jesus of the fourth gospel does not teach in the form of the wise sayings we are familiar with from the other three. He gives lengthy speeches in which an idea is developed by careful verbal movements: forward, backward, forward again, like the steps of a minuet. John's Jesus has second sight; he can read people's hearts. He is in a state of constant communing with God his Father. He continually looks for belief in himself as a true teacher sent from God. Whoever looks on him in faith as he is lifted up from earth—and this for John means both crucifixion and resurrection—will possess the life of the final age.

It is tempting to say that John has changed completely the character of Jesus of Nazareth. The others were content to report him as he was. John has "theologized" him. Worse still, he has divinized him, made a man who was a Jewish *hasid* into the image of God. Yet, a hard look at the other three gospels reveals that they each did something quite like this, even if it is not so immediately evident. All four interpreted the person of Jesus to their readers, and all saw him as someone unique in respect to Israel's God. John's distinction was that he heightened the proximity of this man to God by making him share in all of God's secrets, much like wisdom as the confidant of the LORD in the later biblical books. The appearance given was Greek philosophical or pagan, as if there existed an authentic world of ideas that underlay the elusive manifestations of them in time. Jesus comes close to being a heavenly messenger from Olympus, like Hermes in the guise of a man.

The appearance of the fourth gospel proves deceptive. It is at root a profoundly Jewish piece of writing of the type known as *midrash*. It elaborates on the career of an individual for a pious purpose. The gospel puts speeches on his lips and contrives deeds for his days. Once the basic representation of Jesus has been chosen, all else flows.

In a prologue that is like a preliminary sketch of a portrait to be painted later, John shows a man come into the world whom some accepted and some did not. He was very much a man of "flesh," yet an embodiment of the "word" that was present to God in the beginning. The word came as flesh by a deed of God, the same God who was responsible for people's believing in this word of wisdom. Neither blood nor carnal desire nor humanity's willing it lay behind this begetting of a new race of believers. It was the work of God.

Close scrutiny of John's gospel reveals that although he claims early that something of God came as the man Jesus, God and Jesus are always distinct. Jesus addresses God in the normal human way, that is, as if God were a reality of unbounded holiness other than the speaker. God is God for John. He has a son of his special love, now fully human, whom he knew and had with him before sending him. He means to endow him, after he has suffered, with the glory that was originally his. When this son is no longer on the scene, a spirit of truth will be sent to remind believers of all that Jesus revealed about the Father. The scheme is one of a twofold activity in the world of that God no one has ever seen. First, a mortal man conveys the terms of God's will for the human race by obeying him in everything. Then, a heavenly guide, a counselor or consoler, directs into the path of truth those who would be obedient like him. Both Jesus and this "other paraclete" participate fully in the reality of divinity.

Except for the matter of full participation in the divine life, it is all very Jewish and biblical. As Greek drama it fails, for the gods of the Greeks do not die. The prophets do. So does Jesus.

Half of John's gospel is a book of signs put forward to encourage the reader to believe in Jesus. The other half is a book about his glory, which any casual onlooker might call his shame. The author makes clear from the outset who the central figure of his narrative is to him. He uses Jesus' early discovery by his close followers as the occasion to list a variety of titles. Segments of the Jewish community—some committed to Jesus, some not—have heard of the central importance of a lamb of God, a teacher to come, an anointed one or messiah, a son of Joseph from Nazareth, a son of God, a king of Israel, a son of man.[14] John's point will be that all of these are the one person. They are he whose earthly days and death and glory (glory in death) John now means to tell.

It might be in order at this point to share a few of the many prose poems contained in the fourth gospel. Like Moses' discourses in Deuteronomy or the sermon of the Buddha in the deer park at Banaras, they are a faith literature. They assume faith and seek to increase it.

> I solemnly assure you,
> no one can see the reign of God
> unless he is begotten from above. . . .
> Flesh begets flesh,
> spirit begets spirit. . . .
> The wind blows where it will.
> You hear the sound it makes
> but you do not know where it comes from
> or where it goes.
> So it is with everyone begotten of the spirit.[15]

"Flesh" means here unaided humanity, not corporeal nature and certainly not the sex passion. Spirit is all that is of God, especially

---

14. See Jn 1:35-51   15. Jn 3:3, 6, 8

God as giving life to the world. Darkness and light, lies and truth, are roughly equivalent to flesh and spirit:

Everyone who practices evil
hates the light;
he does not come near it
for fear his deeds will be exposed.
But he who acts in truth
comes into the light,
to make clear that
his deeds are done in God.[16]

Jesus is always the divine emissary who has come from God with a complete message:

The one whom God has sent
speaks the words of God;
he does not ration his gift of spirit.
The Father loves the son
and has given everything over to him.[17]

The man Jesus delights in the task he has been given: "Doing the will of him who sent me and bringing his work to completion is my food."[18] Like a good craftsman, his eyes never stray from God, the master artisan. Jesus is trustworthy because he is not self-seeking:

I solemnly assure you,
the son cannot do anything by himself—
he can only do what he sees the Father doing. . . .
I cannot do anything of myself.
I judge as I hear,
and my judgment is honest
because I am not seeking my own will
but the will of him who sent me.[19]

Jesus, himself elevated by cross and resurrection, will elevate others:

---

16. Jn 3:20–21   17. Jn 3:34–35   18. Jn 4:34   19. Jn 5:19, 30

No one can come to me
unless the Father who has sent me draw him;
I will raise him up on the last day.[20]

He is, above all, a witness to the truth:

You are the one who is saying I am a king.
The reason I was born,
the reason why I came into the world,
is to testify to the truth.
Anyone committed to the truth hears my voice.[21]

Are these the words of Jesus or the theology of John? John, for one, would be stunned to learn that anyone supposed there could be a difference.

---

20. Jn 6:44   21. Jn 18:37

12

The
Storyteller

JESUS TOLD STORIES. THAT IS THE ONE THING THAT WE KNOW
best about him, that and how he died. His stories are often brief
and clear; occasionally they are long and puzzling. Sometimes a
tale will contain an outrageous detail or two that makes the hearer
sit up and take notice. In Jesus' stories, virtue is not always re-
warded. At times the story ends with the stage strewn with corpses,
like a bloody day in the amphitheater at Epidauros or
Shakespeare's Globe.

Storytellers get half their reward out of entertaining people.
That does not mean that they are seeking to amuse, but that they
do intend to give pleasure. A story might go:

> There once was a man down home who decided to divorce his
> wife. The judge prodded him with questions as to why. Finally
> the man said "Your Honor, I've got to. She jes' talks and talks
> and talks." "About what?" "Well, Judge, she don't say."

A story has to be interesting to make anyone repeat it. That means that the story contains enough details to arouse interest, but not enough to kill it. The extra detail of no consequence adds spice; multiplied details ruin the stew. The trick is to keep an audience with you to the end.

The end of Jesus' stories usually comes soon. He was a verbal hit-and-run artist. He painted a quick picture, then moved on. Here are some of his more graphic images, short of the level of stories:

If they were to keep silence,
I tell you the very stones would cry out. . . .[1]

What did you go out to see in the desert,
a reed swayed by the wind. . . ?[2]

Can a blind man lead the blind?
Will not both fall into a ditch. . . ?[3]

The gate that leads to destruction is wide,
the road is clear and many choose to travel it.[4]

Jesus held attention by featuring disparity:

Do you pick grapes from thornbushes
or figs from prickly plants. . . ?[5]

Let the dead bury their dead;
come away and proclaim the kingdom of God.[6]

He did not hesitate to evoke images out of his listeners' past, as in the familiar reference to Elijah's call of Elisha: "Whoever puts his hand to the plow but keeps looking back is unfit for the reign of God."[7]

These sayings are not works of unparalleled genius. The last is strictly paralleled genius—from the Bible, like much that is attributed to Jesus: "Elisha left the oxen, ran after Elijah, and said, 'Let me bid my father and mother goodbye, and I will follow you.'"[8] Elijah sent him back, but when Elisha returned he

1. Lk 19:40   2. Lk 7:24   3. Mt 15:14   4. Mt 7:13   5. Mt 7:16
6. Lk 9:60   7. Lk 9:62   8. 1 Kgs 19:20

slaughtered his oxen, burned the dismembered plow, cooked the meat over a fire, and gave the food to his people to eat. When a storyteller can count on his listeners' knowing a story like that, it makes the task much easier. Popular memory held an inexhaustible stock of tales for the Jew.

The heart of the Jewish tale is metaphor. New wine bursts old skins, houses built on sand come down in the winter rains. This is like this, that is like that, and the less a thing needs spelling out the better. A comparison from any sphere is acceptable, but the closer to people's experience, the deeper the impression it makes.

Jesus never told riddles or conundrums. We don't know why. He never told a fable with talking animals or trees. He had one-character stories and two and three; after that, everyone else was part of the chorus. None of his characters were people you could identify. Only one person in all the parables has a name, the beggar Lazarus, and that name is suspect of having crept into the story long after Jesus told it.

None of Jesus' stories is about himself. There is one possible exception, a tale about some avaricious tenant farmers, but even that tale was probably allegorized by the evangelists' source. The tenants thrash a succession of agents sent by the landowner to collect the revenues due him. Finally, they jump on the owner's son in a fit of greed: "They seized and killed him and dragged him outside the vineyard."[9] Jesus might have told such a story, stopping there. It could have been about a succession of ancient empires and Israel the son, the inheritor of everything God possesses. Ezekiel and Daniel have a number of images like that: a succession of beasts or statues, and finally Israel, always the last, always in human form.

If that is the kind of tale he told in the parable of the tenants, the gospel writers did not leave it alone. They cast it in such a way that you almost have to conclude that the first agents beaten and killed were the prophets, and the last one Jesus the son. The conclusions that Mark and Luke tack on, put on the lips of Jesus, confirm the impression that that is the way they understand the parable:

> What do you suppose the owner of the vineyard will do? He will come and destroy those tenants and turn his vineyard over to others.

9. Mk 12:8

The man who falls on that [rejected] stone [of Psalm 118, Israel] will be smashed to pieces. It will make dust of anyone it falls on.[10]

The chief hitch is that Jesus tells no other story in which he is the central character. More to the point, perhaps, he does not tell any allegories, if we look with care at the thrust of all his stories.

An allegory is a sustained metaphor in which something stands for something else in every case, both character and incident. Mark turns Jesus' story of the sower and his seed into an allegory. Matthew follows him in doing the same. They come close to ruining it, not by the allegorizing but by the moralizing. Jesus stayed away from that. He was interested in a moral, all right, but for much higher stakes. His concern was no less than the salvation of his Jewish people as a people.

Someone has observed, "No one would crucify a teacher who told pleasant stories to enforce prudential morality." That remark goes on the assumption that Jesus met his end as a result of the stories he told. Is there anything to support this view? There could be something to it. When you strip away what the early followers of Jesus did to accommodate his parables to their circumstances—usually making them tales of perseverance until his final coming in judgment—you find that he had one major theme. If you listen hard enough, you cannot miss what he is up to. The one thing he kept saying in a hundred different ways was: the losers will be winners and the winners will be losers. God reads everything differently from the way we do. To find out how differently, you have to make a radical choice.

The theme he kept playing variations on was the reign of God. Jesus' major concern was who would be a part of this majestic rule, and how. His parables invited listeners to discover the alignment of the various characters in the tale. There were always two outlooks, two sides. The listener was invited to pick a side. Jesus never did the choosing for anyone. He stopped each story abruptly, leaving the hearer with the burden of choice. The genius of the technique was that you had to identify with someone in the tale. It

10. Mk 12:9; Lk 20:18; cf. Zech 12:3

was not immediately evident why you should wish to identify with any of them. Black hats and white hats, the sinners and the saints—that would be too easy. Who listens to a second tale when the game is a giveaway the first time? This storyteller kept them guessing.

Jesus worked up a number of tales in which both sides were a little scruffy. That started his listeners thinking. An easy and a false way to get what he was after was to pick the chief authority figure in the story and call him God. Jesus sometimes upset the formula by putting a tyrant or a crook in the role of number one: a king or wealthy sheikh, for example, who threw a party. Jesus then had him take murderous revenge on the little people who stepped out of line. That put you on notice. If you had been paying attention to the way he pictured God all along, you would know that God could not be the vengeful despot in the story. God would be Israel's judge, all right, but not in a petty or cruel way.

The notion of two outcomes was a standard feature in most of Jesus' parables. Someone was always making it and someone was not. What must have dawned on people gradually was that, as conventional edifying tales went, the wrong people were succeeding and the right people getting left. He taught a morality of real justice, not stereotyped justice. He had a firm grasp on the way things are. His "haves" and "have nots" were such that only a God who saw deep into the human heart could choose between them. It was a matter of what it was important to have.

Moreover, and this was the real feature of his teaching in parables, he asked people to choose as if they themselves were God. The simplest unlettered peasant was being told: Don't let anyone decide for you what is right or wrong; you must do the choosing.

One trap easy to fall into is the supposition that Jesus had in mind some providential scheme in which Jews—observant Jews—were the losers and gentiles were the winners. A person can deduce that this is the point of the parable about the laborers in the vineyard,[11] or the man who sowed weeds in the wheat,[12] or the two sons,[13] or the fish in the dragnet.[14] The trouble with that theory is,

---

11. See Mt 20:1–16   12. See Mt 13:24–30   13. See Mt 21:28–31
14. See Mt 13:47–49

one needs to be a gentile who thinks he (she) knows how things worked out in history for it to make any sense to you. Also, you have to ignore a clear fact of the gospels, that Jesus was talking to fellow Jews all the time. He was not teaching people who were not there, or teaching about people who were not there at the time but would read about it later. His whole reign-of-God concern was one he shared with a people that shared it with him. The gentile world, by and large, had never heard of it, or if it had, wrote it off as mad Jewish dreaming. This is to say that the evangelists surely added a church vs. non-church bite to Jesus' parables, but their community of believers was not exclusively gentile nor was its opposition exclusively Jewish.

The reign of God was a dream to this storyteller but it was not madness. It was what God was all about, what life was about, what being Jewish was about. An easy way to dismiss this reign of God is to call it "eschatological," meaning wild, end-of-the-world stuff. The whole concept has been called visionary, and Jesus a seer who died in disappointment when his vision did not come true.

The question is: Who can be sure that it did not come true? If his dream was one of a clearly discernible new epoch that would overtake him, then obviously he must have died disappointed. As a messiah, Jewish-style, Jesus was a flat failure. "The messianic age will be this, it will be that," popular teachers kept saying. He never came close to calling himself a messiah. After his death his followers seemed to think that it was a splendid way to describe him, who he was and yet would be at "the end." But his sights were much lower than that—or much higher. It all depended on whether you followed him. If you did, messiah was the most modest claim you would make for him.

Here are some illustrations of what that reign meant to him. It is a fairly hard-headed outlook. It is not especially mythical:

> Believe me when I say that tax-gatherers and prostitutes are entering into the reign of God before you. . . .[15]

> I assure you, the present generation will not pass away until all this takes place. . . .[16]

---

15. Mt 21:31   16. Mt 24:34

What comparison shall we use for the reign of God? What image will represent it? It is like mustard seed which, when planted in the soil, is the smallest of all the earth's seeds. Yet once it is sown, it springs up to become the largest of shrubs, with branches big enough for the birds of the sky to build nests in its shade. . . .[17]

This is an evil age. It seeks a sign. But no sign will be given it except the sign of Jonah.[18]

Jonah's sign was that of a prophet whose own people did not listen to him, while the heathen Ninevites did. Later, the gospel writers added the detail of the three days in the whale's belly as a sign of Christ's resurrection, but that is not the primitive "sign of Jonah." The resistance of the community of believers is. Jesus tells stories of a God who is patient up to a point:

"For three years now I have come in search of fruit on this fig tree and found none. Cut it down. Why should it clutter up the ground?" In answer, the man said, "Sir, leave it here another year, while I hoe around it and manure it; then perhaps it will bear fruit. If not, then it shall be cut down."[19]

His was a dream about a new Jewish people and even a new human race drawn from anywhere and nowhere; about a tatterdemalion army that recognized its chance and took it. Long afterwards, his disciples worked out a theory to account for why he had not been followed in great numbers. They read Isaiah to the effect that he taught an in-group clearly, but the great mass of hearers he taught in parables so that they would neither hear nor understand.[20]

Bizarre! Mark had a straighter, earlier version of the facts: "By means of many such parables he taught them in a way they could understand."[21]

---

17. Mk 4:30–32   18. Lk 11:29   19. Lk 13:7–9   20. See Mt 13:10–15
21. Mk 4:33

13

The
Truth-Teller

THE JESUS OF WHOM MIRACLES ARE REPORTED, THE MAN OF mystical prayer and utter trust in God, is the same as the speaker of puzzling utterances and challenging tales. This man of compassion who is fully dedicated to the coming of God's reign is none other than the one to whom a variety of high titles is attributed in the accounts of his earthly days. He lived in memory because his sayings and his deeds were remembered. His deeds matched his sayings, and this is a matter of great importance. If he had one message about the way to act, it was that one's actions should always be consistent with one's speech.

He taught: "Say 'Yes' when you mean 'Yes' and 'No' when you mean 'No.' Anything beyond that is from the evil one."[1] He

---

1. Mt 5:37

told his hearers that, while Moses' law forbade taking a false oath and required making good every pledge to the Lord, they were not to swear at all.[2] This suggestion was doubtless related to some of the substitute words for God's name in use at the time. Matthew reports "By heaven!" and "By Jerusalem!" as we might say "By Christopher!" or "By Gosh!"[3] More to the point, there was evidently the custom of weaseling out of one's word by maintaining that one had sworn only by the earth or by one's head, hence was not bound by the pledge so vigorously sworn to.[4] Nothing, after all, had been sworn to "By the Holy One of Israel." Jesus pointed out dryly that since the universe was God's property it came to pretty much the same thing. But his chief concern was the cheapening of the spoken word. A person who could not be trusted in speech could not be trusted in anything.

The important thing for Jesus was to make outward behavior and inward disposition conform: "When you fast, do not look glum like the actors. They change the appearance of their faces so that others may see they are fasting. I assure you, they are already repaid."[5] Jesus was all for grooming hair and washing the face if one had decided to be abstemious at table. What he could not abide was a holy show.

Where would he have stood on the no-makeup-on-principle people, shaven-headed monks and woolly-headed hippies, people in contour-covering habits or with crosses prominently hanging from their necks? Aside from being amused he probably would have been silent. If they acted out their costumes faithfully, he would not have a word to say. In principle he let people live their lives. But let the baggy dress, the plaited hair, the clerical collar, or the blue jeans with patches say one thing and behavior say another, and the thunder would roll. "If you want to look gloomy, be gloomy," he might have said. Don't talk "joy in the Lord" and look like death warmed over.

Beware of performing religious acts for people to see. Otherwise expect no recompense from your heavenly Father. When

---

2. See Mt 5:33–34; Lv 19:12; Nm 30:3   3. See Mt 5:34–35
4. See Mt 5:35–36   5. Mt 6:16

you give alms, blow no trumpets in synagogues or streets like actors seeking applause. Indeed, I tell you, they have had their reward. When you give alms, do not let your left hand know what your right hand is doing. Keep quiet about your acts of mercy and your Father will just as quietly repay you.[6]

Jesus was deeply committed to the idea of the righteousness of God. "Justness" might be a better way to say it. In Hebrew it was *tsedaka*; a just man was a *tsaddik*. A major difference between Jesus and the proponents of certain patterns of piety abroad, as Matthew interpreted him, was that he wanted a God-like holiness in whoever claimed a share in the justice of God, a righteousness that surpassed prevailing practice.[7] He was not, of course, alone in this among the teachers of his time. He put the matter boldly: "You must be perfect [be fully mature? possess integrity?] as your heavenly Father is perfect."[8] The failures of professed teachers of the way of righteousness were almost an obsession with him, in the only reports on his teaching we have. In a reference to the eight days of Passover, when houses had to be rid of every crumb of bread containing yeast, he said:

Be on the lookout against the yeast of the Pharisees and the Sadducees.[9]

The scribes and the Pharisees have succeeded Moses as teachers; therefore do and observe everything they tell you but do not follow their example.[10]

The concluding part of Matthew contains charges so scorching that it is legitimate, as we have indicated (Chapter 3), to wonder how much of it Jesus spoke and how much was colored by the tensions of Matthew's day:

Woe to you scribes and Pharisees, you frauds! You shut the doors of the kingdom of God in men's faces, neither entering yourselves nor admitting those who are trying to enter. . . . You pay tithes on mint and herbs and seeds while neglecting the weightier matters of the law, justice and mercy and good

---

6. Mt 6:1–4   7. See Mt 5:20   8. Mt 5:48   9. Mt 16:6   10. Mt 23:2

faith. . . . You are like whitewashed tombs, beautiful to look
at on the outside but inside full of filth and dead men's bones.
You present a holy exterior to view while hypocrisy and evil
fill you within.[11]

Christians have always reveled in this kind of declamation.
Perhaps this is because of the ambivalence by which language
directed against long-dead Jews can be used by Christian preachers
to strike at their own religious power-class. This double accusation
of the "other" could easily comprise a Christian "pharisaism," as
the dictionary regrettably defines it. But to profit by such ambivalence is the very opposite of the spirit of Jesus. He called a spade a
spade, not a horticultural instrument. He never favored naming
one target and slyly taking aim at another.

It is especially interesting that priests did not fall under Jesus'
verbal censure in the gospels that have come down to us, even
though they were the class seemingly more responsible for his
downfall than lawyers or teachers.[12] One wonders whether the
"woes" spoken by Jesus, if delivered against priests, would have
been a feature of Matthew's gospel if the office of priesthood had
already developed in the church in his time. One likewise wonders
how strong a feature of Christian rhetoric Jesus' hypothetical anti-
priest tirades would have become, given the subsequent emergence
of the office of priest.

The importance of this speculation is that anyone misses
Jesus' point entirely if he uses Jesus' words as weapons against anyone other than himself. They are to be taken as directed to the self,
or else they are perverted. Hypocrisy is not the prerogative of the
highly placed. The lowest-circumstanced among us is capable of it.
Hypocrisy is the natural expression of what is meanest in us all.

We need to ask who of us is meant when Jesus says the
following:

If a person says to his father or mother, "Any support you
might have had from me is *korban*" (that is, dedicated to
God), he need do nothing for his father or mother.[13]

---

11. Mt 23:13, 23, 27–28   12. See Lk 22:2, 66; 23:13   13. Mk 7:11–12

The answer is: anyone who cheats on taxes, who allows reasons to stand in church courts or rabbinical courts that are no real reasons, who says something upright to cover something base. The ancient scribe and Pharisee are not the offender against Jesus' standards so much as anyone in any age who professes belief in him and does not act in his spirit. Anyone is capable of nullifying God's word in favor of the traditions that have been handed on. Therefore Jesus is addressing no single class when he says:

> How accurately Isaiah prophesied against you hypocrites when he wrote, "This people pays me lip service but their heart is far from me. Empty is the reverence they do me because they teach as dogmas human precepts."[14]

There is scarcely a man or woman alive who does not, at some time or other, disregard God's commandment and cling to human tradition.[15] Jesus is a voice over the ages—not the only voice but a powerful one—telling us to do as we say and say as we do. T.S. Eliot paraphrased him well in citing as the ultimate treason, "doing the right thing for the wrong reason."

A disreputable figure in one of Jesus' stories makes a personal audit when he learns he has been caught at his thieving and is about to be fired:

> What shall I do next? My employer is sure to dismiss me. I cannot dig ditches. I am ashamed to go begging. I have it! Here is a way to make sure that people will take me into their houses when I am let go![16]

So he sets about his felonious little plan. Jesus is not especially interested in the man's morality, for purposes of his story. Although he certainly would have favored a change of heart in him, he would at the same time have commended his consistency. Jesus was above all an apostle of consistent behavior. We know, by contrast, the way in which another well-known character in a parable is viewed. With unbowed head, this observant prays publicly in the temple area:

---

14. Mk 7:6–7   15. See Mk 7:8   16. Lk 16:3–4

I give you thanks, O God, that I am not like the rest of men—
grasping, crooked, adulterous—or even like this tax-gatherer.
I fast twice a week. I pay tithes on all I possess.[17]

There was another character in the story who kept his distance, not
even daring to raise his eyes to heaven. All he did was beat his
breast and say, "O God, be merciful to me a sinner." Jesus calls this
one just before God, the other one not.

In a way, the stereotypes are a little too neat: Pharisee and
tax-gatherer. One thing we can be sure of is Jesus' equal contempt
for the tax-gatherer if his humility is a pose. That, Jesus could not
have endured. For him God is the one who justifies. How a man
stands in his own eyes, he is free to say, but what the ultimate verdict is, is for God to say.

Jesus praises John the Baptizer as greater than any person
born of woman. He does not sway in the wind like a reed nor dress
luxuriously like a hanger-on at court.[18] Day after day he speaks the
truth. Jesus knows no higher calling.

When Peter will not hear of the bitter end that Jesus suspects
lies in store for him, he rebukes Peter sharply: "Get out of my sight,
you satan! You are not judging by God's standards but by man's."[19]
The standard is always the same: the reality that is or must be.
Neither soft talk nor flight from reality is any part of Jesus' settlement with life. Whoever would preserve life—meaning the integrity of selfhood—will lose it; whoever loses life will preserve it.
"What profit does a person show who gains the whole world and
destroys self in the process? What can anyone give in exchange for
one's life?"[20]

Mark says early that this relentless, honest speech is what
won Jesus a hearing: "The people were spellbound by his teaching
because he taught with authority. . . ."[21] Some have taken this
authority to be the power of God, and they are probably right. The
very force of Jesus' words would, however, suffice. They stood on
their own. They commanded a hearing.

---

17. Lk 18:11–12   18. See Lk 7:28, 24–25   19. Mk 8:33
20. Mk 8:36–37   21. Mk 1:22

One problem that arose long ago has to do with Jesus' concern for reward. He seems not to be interested in the worth of the human deed for its own sake, as a Greek philosopher might be. Act thus and your heavenly Father will act so. Do this and expect that. His mentality has put him, for many, in the second rank of moralists. They are repelled by the motivations he holds out. The humanlike God of Jesus strikes them as less than sublime, a cosmic wielder of the carrot and the stick.

It is not the speech of Jesus but the religion of Israel, from which he does not depart, that needs exposition here. For centuries it had viewed relationships with other human beings as humanity's principal problem in life. This was the norm for service of God. The ideal remedy for the human condition was a state of affairs where wickedness is overcome and individuals treat one another properly. The God from whom all life had come was seen as having a personal stake in this ethical salvation that Israel sought. God cared, and cared passionately, how people chose. He was as necessarily in on the outcome of their choices as he was on the choices themselves.

It was unthinkable for Jesus to depart from the Jewish conviction that the deed was not an isolated good, perfect in itself. It had consequences for humans and consequences for God—the two sets of consequences in a necessary relation. Jesus features both. Sin and right-doing had unavoidable outcomes.

In identifying Jesus as a lover of truth, one is tempted to regret the fact that the gospels find a foil for his fulminations against insincerity in the scribes and Pharisees. Was he as singleminded in his opposition to these observants *en bloc* as his followers of a half-century later were toward their contemporary opposite numbers? The best scholars think not. At the same time, we will never know how penetrating the message of Jesus against hypocrisy would have been if he did not have someone as a foil in the gospels.

We can only say that dissembling and deceiving are so clearly the opposite of all that Jesus stands for that anyone who claims the title Christian and acts the hypocrite is perverting the gospel as thoroughly as can be done.

14

The
Man of
Compassion

IF THE MAIN THRUST OF JESUS' TEACHING WAS TRUST IN
God, the chief incentive he provided his hearers to take him
seriously was his compassion. We tend to call it empathy nowadays but it is the same thing. It means "suffering with." The notion
underlying both words is not that all of life is suffering, as a
Buddhist might maintain, but that there is suffering in all of life. In
the Bible and the Qur'an, the person who helps you live best is the
one who shows a willingness to suffer with you. Even God the
merciful is compassionate in that sense.

There are such realities as failure of nerve, the courting of
martyrdom, unhealthy masochism. By admitting that there is suffering in life that must be accepted, one does not thereby say a kind
word for any of these. The fight against poverty and disease makes
steady progress, yet suffering continues. Suffering is the traveling
companion of hunger, of the displacement of populations, of

genocide. On a psychic level we speak of alienation and rejection and their correlatives, anxiety and fear. Those terms describe modern realities. As a blanket term, the one that does it best is "suffering."

Compassion, quite simply, is the capacity to put yourself in someone else's shoes, since all are sufferers.

If the mood is condescending, however unconscious this may be, a certain disqualification sets in by that fact. No one is the patron of another—not even the benign patron—and at the same time compassionate.

Pity is a rich emotion, but it has one further step to go before it becomes compassion. The one who extends pity must be put totally in the place of the other.

Jesus was compassionate in accepting prostitutes, rent-gougers, and collaborationists for what they were. He conveyed to them that he felt their pain. The evidence is not much in quantity but the conclusion is inescapable. He consistently sought the company of losers. No moralizing words of his are recorded beyond the admonition to "sin no more." We are told of certain sinners who were changed. We have this admonition after the change, none before.

It does not help much to praise Jesus for having had a comfortable villager's life that he left for insecurity. Not even pointing out that he died hard in a death that a little compromise might have avoided is useful. For believers, Jesus' itinerant lifestyle and violent end belong in the category of providence. Yet these surely were not without the element of chance. We assume that he accepted both way of life and exit from life; we do not know that he directly chose either. We are only sure that he pursued a goal that entailed them. We have far better evidence for his spirit of compassion: the fact that he threw in his lot with people of every type, without recorded comment on the nobility of the venture. He was where people were—in their pain.

We know that Jesus was a teacher who taught in a spirit that invited imitation. Such teachers are normally the last to draw close to them those they are trying to reach. The moralist picks up many followers on a principle of common superiorty to the "unsaved." People at every level of society felt close to Jesus, yet he seems to have had no such recruitment principle as that.

Many were women. Foolish women do not recognize the men who despise them, while wise women know the men who ac-

cept them. There were a few intellectuals of his acquaintance that
we know about. There were some aristocrats of property. We are
told of gormandizers and tipplers but also many ordinary people in
cities and towns. The physically disabled whom the busily healthy
had forgotten were among his followers. So were the demented, a
class embarrassing to every society. He drew children close. We do
not know how any other male figure of antiquity felt about
children aside from getting sons. Criminals, or at least the con-
victed, were among his associates. Finally, there were ordinary
peasants by the thousands who had no hope either in this world or
in the "age to come."

It is possible to interpret the entire phenomenon of Jesus as
one that took place in a society in ferment that exploded. The
general run of his listeners could not have been worse off. He promised a universal upheaval, using biblical speech from the psalms
that featured the beggar on the throne and the power person exposed naked to his enemies. He gained followers, it could be said,
because he promised an end to social oppression.

This solution to the problem of Jesus—namely, viewing him
as a social revolutionary—is attractive. It fits the case of many
popular heroes of a brief season. As we have already hinted,
however, it does not square with his recorded words or deeds.

Unfriendly voices asked him: "Why do you eat and drink
with tax-gatherers and sinners?" He said: "The healthy do not need
a doctor. Sick people do."[1]

When onlookers protested what they thought was a needless
waste of perfume by a woman who anointed him at table, he said:
"Let her alone. Why do you criticize her? She has done me a kindness."[2] In what may be another telling of the same story, where the
woman's reputation is described as unsavory, he responded with a
parable. A money-lender canceled the debts of two who owed him
money, a large sum and a small. Jesus first elicited the response that
the former ought to be the more grateful of the two. Then he said:
"I tell you, her great love is why her many sins are forgiven her.
Little is forgiven a person who has not loved much."[3]

---

1. Lk 5:31   2. Mk 14:6   3. Lk 7:47

Yet it does not appear that people had to conform to any special pattern to qualify for Jesus' compassion. A gentile woman gives a sharp retort in which Jesus as a Jew gets his comeuppance. She knows the claim of Jewish religious superiority. She reminds him of it by asking with heavy irony for scraps for the dog from the master's table. He can only say, "Touché." "For such a reply, be on your way? The demon has left your daughter."[4]

Jesus has no principle of cronyism in the work he is about. He will put himself in anyone's shoes. A reply to his close friends, who are distressed that someone not of their company has been casting out devils in his name must have deflated them completely: "Do not stop him. . . . Anyone who is not against us is with us."[5]

He is moved by the fate of a madman,[6] a widow who has lost her son,[7] a variety of the blind[8] and the paralyzed.[9] We may well ask who would do less if he or she were conscious of a power such as Jesus had? What we cannot know is how his power was related to his compassion. Most people who observe suffering can do little about it. Can it be because they are so little moved by it? Jesus both observed suffering and felt it. He could also therefore heal.

What is not a matter of speculation is Jesus' total availability in the midst of a literal bone-crushing by the crowds that hemmed him in. They kept coming because they thought he cared. And because they were right, because he did care, he stayed with them hour after hour. We assume that the cost in physical exertion was high. What it might have been in mental strain we cannot know, except for what we glean from an occasional phrase: he groaned,[10] he sighed,[11] his frame was shaken.[12] Once, he is reported having been conscious of "power going out from him," like the *mana* of the Melanesians and Polynesians.[13] Paradoxically, he is at his calmest when addressing those who are called "unclean spirit." Of these he rids sufferers by a word of command. If there is any special burden laid upon him by this proximity to evil, we are not told of it.

The compassion of Jesus is better described as corporate than individual. He finds himself surrounded daily by people who

4. Mk 7:29   5. Mk 9:39–40   6. See Mk 9:17–29   7. See Lk 7:11–15
8. See Mk 8:22–26; Jn 9:1–7   9. See Mt 8:5–13; 9:2–8   10. See Mk 7:34
11. See Mk 8:12   12. See Jn 11:33   13. See Mk 5:30

are bent over double, by victims of running sores and withered limbs, by the mute and the deaf. The net effect of all this human misery on him is not depressant. The only charge he levels against anyone—always the onlookers, never the victim—is lack of trust in God. The chief offender is "this generation," which is faithless by definition. It is as if Jesus, faced with mass infirmity, is pressed to plead for a mass faith that will bring humanity strength from outside itself.

Does he ever make an equation between the greed of the rich and the fate of the poor? He does not seem to. He has a preoccupation with the self-centeredness that cuts across social and economic lines. For him, the demon of self-torture is not a class thing. Yet his deepest compassion goes out to the wretched of the earth. His sympathy for the rich, if he has any, is well hidden. Yet wretchedness is never defined simply as poverty. It is a total deprivation in which lack of spiritual resources is paramount. The ordinary discomfort that people endure makes its impact on him: "My heart is moved with pity for the crowd. They have been with me three days now and have nothing to eat. If I send them home hungry, they will collapse on the way."[14] But another kind of distress is uppermost in his thoughts: "At the sight of the crowds he was moved with pity. They were lying prostrate with exhaustion, like sheep without a shepherd."[15]

The phrase is from Ezekiel[16] and Matthew may have supplied it. In the book of the prophet it comes as part of a sharp charge laid at the door of "the shepherds of Israel who have been pasturing themselves."[17] Jesus seemed to be as convinced as Ezekiel that a none too benign neglect underlay the distress of the crowds. His whole effort was to find some nourishment for them to feed on, some water for them to drink.

A movement to restore the law of Moses to the common people was gaining strength at the time Jesus taught. His simplified version of keeping the law must have caused pain to some of the earnest backers of the movement. He seemed to be hawking salvation at cut rates—Bonhoeffer's "cheap grace." Yet the compassion he asked for, like the compassion he showed, was not without its

---

14. Mk 8:2-3   15. Mt 9:36   16. Ez 34:5-6   17. Ez 34:2

price. He had praise for a widow who, donating to the temple treasury, "gave from her want, all that she had to live on."[18]

The ideal that Jesus lived by is probably best conveyed in his stories. A father embraces his son who has gone on the road, living as if there were no tomorrow. He even throws a party for this "dead one who has come back to life."[19] A worthless lout of a debtor throttles a fellow-slave who owes him a tiny sum, after his owner has remitted thousands to him.[20] A Samaritan—to Jesus' listeners a despised class—is compassionate when a priest and a levite will not run the risk of defilement by a corpse.[21] An employer throws equity to the winds and pays laborers who worked a few hours at the same rate as those who worked all day.[22]

These tales convey a spirit, a mood, more than any set of principles.

You help the person who is down. You do not keep a set of books on people. You have the loser uppermost in your thoughts. Suffering is to be found everywhere in life. The work that should compel your highest energies is to relieve it. Death, disease, frenzy, debt—all these describe humanity as victim. Humanity as victor lives, lives whole, celebrates.

From the house that knows compassion there can be heard the sound of music and dancing.[23]

18. Mk 12:44   19. See Lk 15:24   20. See Mt 18:23–35
21. See Lk 10:30–37   22. See Mt 20:1–16   23. See Lk 15:25

15

The
Man of
Trust

Teaching by stories and examples, not by philosophical disquisitions, is the Jewish way. Jesus of Nazareth employed it. He achieved a certain mastery of it, distinguishing himself at the storyteller's art. Some of his statements are brusque, others are shocking. His tales go against the accepted wisdom. He continues to tell them without interruption.

Jesus seems to have liked challenge; he gave it and he got it. His admiring disciples, years after the event, portrayed him as winning every exchange. It is easy to envision what would have been his distress at the embroidered report. The man had a passionate, even a painful regard for the truth. Some disciples of the Pharisees are reported to have said to him once: "Teacher, we know you are a truthful man and teach God's way sincerely. You court no one's favor and do not act out of human respect. Give us your opinion, then, in this case. . . ."[1]

---

1. Mt 22:16–17

Anyone who cannot warm to the livelier exchanges told of him—verbal wrestling matches, like Jacob's with the angel—has not known many Jews. According to the gospels Jesus would rather talk than eat. In this he was a true son of his father Abraham.

What was the talk about? About one thing, chiefly: the way to bring on speedily the reign of Israel's God, her King. Every Jew was interested in that question on some terms. Jesus proposed a single way, the way of trust. Another way to say it is dependence. Reliance. Faith. He did not care what you called it, so long as you practiced it. He went at the question from every possible angle. His teaching was: If you wish to know a little happiness before you die, let God run the world. After you have done that for a while, you can give him a chance at minding you.

The proposal is fairly simple. It has never had an easy time of it, either before Jesus or after him. Most people think it simple-minded. Some say: "Well, that's all right as Oriental quietism, but it isn't Jewish. Read the Bible. You'll see that a Jew has to stay in motion, to strive, to contend." That much is true about the Bible. Jesus never said otherwise. But he seemed all the while to have his eye on a passage from one of David's psalms that he never quoted: "Be still, and know that I am God."[2] His ideal was human activity in a mood of perfect trust.

The story of the Exodus was filled with injunctions to trust. The food gave out, water was scarce, foot-coverings wore thin, yet there was always enough. Not the meat supplies of Egypt, perhaps, those famous "fleshpots" that had nothing to do with sex and everything to do with survival, but there was always enough food on the ground, that mysterious manna, and enough quail exhausted from their flight across the sea. There was a trickle of water "struck from the rock" that came up through the sun-baked mud flats. None of this was a surplus but it was a sufficiency.

The same was true in the famine of Jacob's time and the drought of Elijah's. The Lord always provided, even when none but a lonely patriarch or prophet knew he would. Under siege of Assyria and Babylonia it was the same story. The practical, political counsel given by the various prophets was not always consistent; the exhortation to trust was.

---

2. Ps 46:11

"Make no alliances," was Isaiah's advice to King Ahaz, "he will save you. Trust in him alone." Jeremiah said, "Put up no resistance. Let the Babylonian tide come. Trust only in him."

The Pharisees of Jesus' time were in the mold of Jeremiah; the Zealots were not. The latter proposed taking up arms as a way of liberation from Rome. Jesus argued matters on another level than the various schools of thought around him. If he dealt immediately with the political or economic situation of his time, we do not know about it. We do know that he went to the bottom of things.

Avoid greed in all its forms. A man may be wealthy but possessions do not guarantee him life.[3]

Your Father in heaven knows everything you need. Seek first his rule over you, his way of justice, and all these things will be given you besides.[4]

It was strange advice to give to marginal populations. This was a proletariat, a landless poor whose only commodity was their labor, their lives. They showed no talent for turning it into a weapon against oppressive capital. Jesus did not ask them to. He told them to trust in God.

This advice has caused all kinds of mischief since. The main havoc comes when people who do not trust in God mouth the need for trust, in Jesus' name. On his lips it was believable; he acted as if it were true. He told others to look at the birds of the air and the flowers of the field, and lived the life of an itinerant to show what sense it made.

Trusting in God was not some feature out at the edges of Jesus' teaching; it was the heart and center. This and only this would hasten the reign of God. He thought that the opposite of trust in God was trust in things:

Do not lay up for yourselves an earthly treasure.
    Moth and rust corrode.
    Thieves break in and steal.
Store up instead treasure in heaven
    which neither moth nor rust corrodes

---

3. Lk 12:15   4. Mt 6:32–33

> nor thieves break in and steal.
> Where your treasure is, there your heart is also.[5]

He is reported to have said:

> No man can serve two masters.
>> He will either hate one and love the other
>> or serve one and despise the other.
> You cannot serve both God and money.[6]

The rich man in one of his stories is called a fool for tearing down his barns and building new ones to store his grain in. He said to himself: "Relax! You have good things in store for years to come." That night he died.

The story is over. Jesus simply asks his hearers: Who is to get it all?[7]

He has another tale of rich and poor in which a beggar lies at the gate of a wealthy man who dresses elegantly and dines well. The beggar's scabs are indistinguishable from his dirty wrappings. His diet is selective, what the dogs do not get first. Yet he kept his honor through it all. It is made clear, at any rate, that the rich man did not keep his. One is left to wonder what other ways there are to get rich.

When both are dead, an abyss is fixed between them. Says Abraham to the rich man: "My son, remember that you had good things in life while Lazarus was in misery. Now he has found consolation here but you have found torment."[8]

A tale like this raises the question whether Jesus was a radical social reformer. Did he seethe with indignation at the lot of the poor? It seems as if the answer is no. One senses that he would put Lazarus in torment just as readily if the beggar had put his trust in scraps from the table. Jesus was against poor fools as well as rich fools. He just thought the percentage of poor fools did not run so high.

He said once: "How hard it will be for the rich to enter into the realm of God. It is easier for a camel to go through a needle's eye."[9] And another time:

---

5. Mt 6:19–21   6. Mt 6:24   7. Lk 12:16–20   8. Lk 16:25
9. Lk 18:24–25

Woe to you rich. Your consolation is now.
Woe to you full bellies. You shall go hungry.
Woe to you laughers. You shall weep in your grief.[10]

It sounds at times as though he hated the rich. But when you examine all that he had to say about them, it seems that he rather felt
sorry for them. They were in trouble, a kind of trouble he did not
have. The poor, he seemed to think, were in better condition. At
least they could be. He held out the hope of a drastic change in their
fortunes. But to hear Jesus talk, even now they had the best of it.

"Sell all you have and give to the poor," he said once to a
member of the ruling class. The fellow was not ready for it: "Hearing this, the man became sad, for he was very rich."[11] In *Poor
Richard's Almanac*, the fool and his money are soon parted. Not in
the gospel. There the fool acts like the real rich. He hangs on to it.
He is parted from it only by death.

Jesus was not against comfort, so far as we can tell. He was
against encumbrance. Ties made him nervous. He recruited for the
open road; he invited people to the road of the spirit: "Give to the
poor and . . . you will have treasure in heaven [meaning, "with
God"]. Then come, follow me."[12]

He has no kind words to say for protecting one's good
name. He never praises providing for the future. He is silent about
taking ordinary precautions. It is all: "Stop worrying. Do without.
Let go." The line that probably sums up his outlook best is: "Freely
have you received, freely give."[13] Nowadays we might say, in a
lyric from the thirties: "Let's lend it, spend it, send it rolling along."

The interesting thing is, you can imagine Jesus in disbelief
and anger at finding someone who had dispossessed himself totally
and trusted in that! He was not for relying on a negative factor like
not having. He certainly did not favor a positive one like "the
boundless resources of the self." For Jesus the Jew, a person's
completion lay outside the self. It lay in another whom no eye
could see.

The name of the game was not dispossession. It certainly was
not forcible expropriation. It was perfect trust, trust in another.

---

10. Lk 6:24–25   11. Lk 18:23   12. Lk 18:22   13. Mt 10:8

Jesus' disciples said to him once, "Increase our faith." He answered: "If you had faith the size of a mustard seed, you could say to this tree, 'Be uprooted and transplanted into the sea,' and it would obey you."[14] That counsel was not based on a conviction of harmony in the universe or even psychic power. The faith he was talking about was in someone who could throw trees around and did it regularly. Jesus never suggested mistrust of self. He constantly recommended trust in another. Whether mistrust of self was a requirement for trust in God was something the individual had to decide. In the case of this "quietist" teacher, hesitancy, inaction, and uncertainty about the self do not seem to have had much place.

For Jesus, the ultimate determiner of human affairs was God. He thought of God as one might think of a father in a large kinship family: dedicated to the needs of his clan, protective, providing. In our culture this is often the mother's role.

In Jesus' view of this father's care, those who asked got. There was also punishment for the wrongdoer: "Do not fear those who deprive the body of life but cannot destroy the soul. Rather, fear him who can destroy both body and soul in Gehenna."[15]

Worry cannot add a minute to your life span.[16] Clothes, food, drink—these are matters that God cares more about than any human being knows how.[17]

The unbelievers are always running after these things. Your heavenly Father knows all that you need. . . . Enough of worrying about tomorrow. Let tomorrow take care of itself. Today has enough troubles of its own.[18]

The model for care is the parent who cares, even the foolish parent:

Would one of you hand his son a stone when he asks for a loaf, or a snake when he asks for a fish? If you, with all your sins, know how to give good things to your children, how much more will your heavenly Father give good things to anyone who asks.[19]

---

14. Lk 17:5-6   15. Mt 10:28   16. See Mt 6:27   17. See Mt 6:28-31
18. Mt 6:32, 34   19. Mt 7:9-11

God as trickster, God as frustrater of human desires, is someone Jesus knows nothing of. People first have to get their desires in order, make sure they recognize their own needs. After that, a course of action is easy:

Ask and you shall receive.
Seek and you shall find.
Knock and it shall be opened to you.[20]

Jesus was not in search of a race of craven suppliants. He was looking for realists. He did not recruit beggars looking for scraps from a rich man's table, meaning a God who lets a few crumbs drop if people will crawl. There was nothing craven in the outlook of this teacher. He crawled for no one; he suggested crawling to no one.

He was convinced he knew the One things came from. He thought that everybody would be happier if they acknowledged the fact.

The German philosopher Feuerbach wrote, "The weak have a strong God." Jesus taught: "The strong are strong because they do not have a weak God." They know where good gifts come from.

---

20. Mt 7:7

16

The
Glutton and
Drunkard

SO FAR AS WE CAN TELL, JESUS ATE WITH ANYBODY WHO
would eat with him. The outcry against "eating with sinners" is so
constant in the gospels that it must testify to some sort of adverse
social sanction. We are handicapped here, as in so many matters,
because we are not sure how far the oral tradition of the rabbis on
table practice had been developed by Jesus' day. The charge of
being compromised by association with the morally depraved is
not in question here. "Sinners" may, of course, have included
thieves or streetwalkers, but it is probably a much broader
technical term to describe nonobservants of the oral law. The
understanding probably was that observance of table customs,
from the dietary prohibitions of the Torah down to the recently
introduced handwashing, would be imperiled if people did not
watch the company they kept.

Jews were never prohibited from eating with gentiles. There was no such nonassociation rule. All the difficulties arose from the circumstances. The tractate *Hagigah* in the Mishnah records that the clothes of peasants (literally, the "people of the land") can make the Pharisees unclean by *midras* (touch or pressure), and that the clothes of Pharisees provide a similar hazard for priests. Two other classes of functionaries in temple sacrifice are named as potential defilers of others with their vesture. Those who "eat of hallowed things" is the description of the ones at the top of the pyramid. The apron of Joseph ben Joezer, the most pious of the priesthood, could defile even *them*.[1] This grading of recipients of defilement must have had some effective meaning while the temple stood. If such were the precautions taken within the ranks of the temple priesthood and beyond, we can see how grievous a threat to purity the ordinary person in a crowd would have been.

The questions raised by menses, semen, and even perspiration were extensive. To them were added the problems of unrinsed hands[2] and unwashed vessels.[3] The tractate *Demai* ("Produce") of the Tosefta reads in one place:

> They receive as a *haber* (table companion) him who takes on himself four things: not to give the priests' portion or tithes to the people of the land, and not to make ready his ritually prepared food in the presence of the people of the land, and to prepare ordinary food in purity. . . . The Sages say:"If he stays as a guest with the people of the land he can still be trustworthy. . . ."[4]

We gather from the gospels that, in the interests of being in the midst of common people, Jesus did not scruple about the prescriptions for purity that were enforced by the rigorists of his time.

He has one saying about eating that stands alone in its potential for offending rabbinic sensibilities. If he uttered it, as alleged, he put himself in opposition to the total scheme of levitical purity regarding foods:

---

1. See *Hagigah* ("The Festal Offering") 2, 7
2. See *ibid.*, 2, 5; 3, 2; *Eduyoth* ("Testimonies") 6, 6
3. See *Kelim* ("Vessels") in its entirety   4. *Demai* 2, 2

"Hear me, all of you, and try to understand. Nothing that enters a man from ouside can make him impure; that which comes out of him, and only that, constitutes impurity. . . . That which enters a man does not penetrate his being, but enters his stomach only and passes into the latrine." Thus did he render all foods clean. He went on: "What emerges from within a man, that and nothing else, is what makes him impure."[5]

It is quite unlikely that Jesus meant to abrogate the food laws of Leviticus 11 by his strong declaration about evil thoughts. That is the conclusion Mark draws from it in the gentile circumstances he is laboring in. Proof of this is Matthew's elimination of the shocking conclusion about "all foods" when he comes to edit Mark. He has Jesus castigate the evils that stem from the mind just as roundly,[6] but end by saying: "As for eating with unwashed hands, that makes no one impure."[7] This leaves us with a memorable utterance of Jesus on genuine evil as contrasted with specious. He probably made it in the context of an argument about the fitness of foods. His gentile followers put the saying to work in support of their practice, which was completely nonobservant.

The technique of argumentation employed in the New Testament is the oldest and best known in religious literature. The context, for the modern mentality, means the terms of the original discussion or usage; the context for the ancients meant what they were attempting to establish.

Many lively verbal encounters reported of Jesus took place at table. Luke says that a company of women who had been cured of various illnesses and evil spirits took care of the itinerants in his company out of their means.[8]

It comes as no surprise that the group is supposed to have had a solemn leave-taking at a meal on the brink of Jesus' arrest. He was condemned and executed at the spring feast of Passover. The first three gospels say that he ate the Passover meal with his companions. He may have done so, but this is impossible to prove. The opposite, in fact, seems likely. The fourth gospel says that he

---

5. Mk 7:14-15, 19-20   6. See Mt 15:19; Mk 7:21-22   7. Mt 15:20
8. See Lk 8:3

was crucified on the day of preparation for the feast. John appears to be factually correct against the first three. This would mean that the latter were using "Passover" in a figurative sense, identifying Jesus with the lamb of sacrifice.

After the temple was destroyed, the Jews accommodated themselves to its absence with remarkable speed by a number of metaphorical interpretations. It is impossible to tell from the Mishnah, compiled around the year 200, that temple sacrifice is no longer a daily occurrence. Similarly, the earliest Christians converted their Jewish meal, commemorative of release from Egypt, into, first, an anticipation of Jesus' return (like Elijah's), and then a retrospective contemplation of the meaning of his death. This table practice of the new community was already stylized by the time it was written up in Paul's first letter to Corinth and the gospels as the "last supper." One proof of this is the similarity of the wording of this event to Jesus' words over the loaves and the fish in multiplying them.

It has been theorized that Jesus and his friends constituted a *ḥaburah* (table fellowship) and as such took their meals, including the final one, commonly. But such a company of *ḥaberim* was a society for the strict observance of ritual cleanliness. No evidence inclines us to describe this as an interest of Jesus. The phenomenon of males traveling together in the Middle East is so commonplace that any suspicion of homosexuality betrays a cultural parochialism. The farthest back we can take the "last supper" phenomenon, besides its naturalness for pilgrims arrived for the week-long feast, is to the minimum company of ten specified for Passover observance. But again, it is less than likely that such was the literal character of the meal.

This question is rendered relatively unimportant by the sacred character of all Jewish meals. The blessedness of the LORD, the "King of the universe," was remembered over broken bread— and wine for those who could afford it. There was, of course, an order (*seder*) of observance at a Passover supper. There was a specified dialogue built around the narrative of deliverance found in Exodus 12. "Why is this night the holiest night of the year?" a son would ask the father, or the youngest male the eldest or leading figure in the group. None of this ritual exchange is reported in the gospels. Neither is there any indication of the lengthy, jolly celebration most Passover suppers turn into. There is silence about the bitter herbs, eggs, and lamb. The one possible exception is *haroseth*, the sweet sauce of nuts and raisins to remind the group of the mortar for the bricks their fathers made. Conceivably this was the contents of the dish into which the betrayer dipped his hand along with Jesus.[9]

Such speculation is idle, however. The Christian meal had been transformed into something quite different by the time it was written up. Mark speaks of "the feasts of Passover and Unleavened Bread"[10] as if they were different from each other. There is, in fact, some indication that the seven days of *matzoth* followed the night of *pesaḥ* as if distinct from it. Luke refers to the two as one, "the feast of Unleavened Bread known as the Passover."[11] This usage is paralleled in Josephus. By the time the book of Exodus was compiled, the two observances had already come together, whatever their previous histories.[12] This development from a spring harvest festival of the Canaanites into a memorial of the mercy of the God of Israel was similar to that of all Jewish observances. It is not surprising that the Passover feast should have had a further development in the midst of a Jewish company such as Jesus' followers, who were convinced they had experienced something new.

Second Isaiah (Chapters 40-55) had written boldly after the exile that the exodus should no longer be commemorated, so striking was God's recent deed of release from Babylonian captivity:

Remember not the events of the past,
     the things of long ago consider not;
See, I am doing something new.
     Now it emerges, do you not perceive it?
In the desert I make a way
     and in the wasteland paths.[13]

His counsel was not heeded. No commemorative feast was developed to outstrip that of Passover. But the mentality countenancing fluidity was there. The followers of Jesus developed a new feast, their Passover, because of the conviction that they had lived through something new.

---

9. See Mt 26:23   10. Mk 14:1   11. Lk 22:1   12. See Ex 12:14–15
13. Is 43:18–19

The central features of the sacred meal of Christians are well known. There is no lamb because Jesus is thought to be that, just as there is no lamb at a Jewish *seder*, only a bone on the plate. Each of the two groups was faced with the problem of the nonexistence of temple sacrifice. Each responded in a different way. While the rabbis kept all the other aspects of the meal alive, the followers of Jesus reduced their symbols of deliverance to the staples of any celebrative meal, bread and wine. Were they influenced in this by the practice the Jewish sectarians at Qumrân by the shores of the Dead Sea? Did the two already share a common mentality of resistance to the sacred slaughter that went on in the temple? None of the preparations for the final meal reported in the gospels lead us to suppose so.[14] The progressive alienation of the Christians from the temple, particularly the Hellenist Jewish-Christian wing of the diaspora, was probably a much more influential factor.

Yet the Qumrân practice is worth recording. The following occurs in a brief document describing the "men of renown" who will serve as the council of the community:

And when they shall gather together for the common table, to eat and to drink new wine, when the common table shall be set for eating and the new wine poured for drinking, let no man extend his hand over the first-fruits of bread and wine before the priest; for it is he who shall bless the first-fruits of bread and wine, and shall be the first to extend his hands over the bread. Thereafter the messiah of Israel shall extend his hand over the bread, and all the congregation of the community shall utter a blessing, each man in the order of his dignity.

It is according to this statute that they shall proceed at every meal at which at least ten men are gathered together.[15]

Jesus and his immediate followers numbered neither priests nor levites that we know of. Some of the former were added to the company shortly, if the book of Acts is to be credited in its report.[16]

---

14. See Mk 14:12, 14–16
15. *The Rule of the Future Congregation (Messianic Rule)*, II
16. See Acts 4:36–37; 6:7

The whole band of his followers soon began to think of itself as priestly, just as the law of Moses called Israel a nation of priests. The similarity of the last supper account to the projection of the future given in the quotation above lies elsewhere. Just as we have in the Qumrân scroll a plan of behavior for the last age, when the messiah of Israel would be in the midst of the community (possible two messiahs—the "priest" may be thought of as a non-kingly messiah)—so in the gospels there is a looking forward on Jesus' part to the final age:

> "I have greatly desired to eat this Passover with you before I suffer. I tell you, I will not eat it again until it is fulfilled in the reign of God." Then taking a cup he offered a blessing in thanks and said: "Take this and divide it among you; I tell you, from now on I will not drink of the fruit of the vine until the coming of the reign of God."[17]

He then proceeds, in Luke, to call the bread in his hands his body and the cup a covenant in his blood that is to be shed "for you." Matthew has the same words of intent not to drink any wine "until I drink it new with you in my father's reign."[18] This vow of abstention is like that of the mother of the nazirite Samson—no wine until a certain matter is accomplished[19]—or Hannah's vow of perpetual nazirite status for her son Samuel.[20] Paul will tell the Corinthians that by eating this bread and drinking this cup they are to proclaim the death of the Lord "until he come."[21] In both approaches to the Christian meal there is the same note of futurity that is found in the Qumrân meal. It is a looking forward by Jesus until something is accomplished, and by Paul until Jesus should come.

This can properly be called expectation of the end, even as the "apocalypse of Isaiah" (Chapters 24-27) had looked forward centuries before to a banquet for all in the final age:

> On this mountain the LORD of hosts
>   will provide for all peoples
> A feast of rich food and choice wines,
>   juicy rich food and pure, choice wines . . . .

---

17. Lk 22:15-18   18. Mt 26:29   19. Jgs 13:4   20. 1 Sam 1:11
21. 1 Cor 11:26

He will destroy death forever,
the LORD God will wipe away
   the tears from every face.[22]

Did Jesus actually have a last supper with his friends, at which he instructed them to think of the bread and wine as himself each time they ate it? It seems clear that there was such a leave-taking meal, and that at it Jesus prayed over food with an eye to what lay ahead for him. Afterward, his followers kept eating such meals centered on him, primarily with an eye to what lay ahead for them but also to what lay behind. Later the order was reversed. Commemoration of his past suffering was stressed over anticipation of his return in glory as the consummation of God's reign. In all of this, Jesus' vow remained paramount. His followers could only have begun to eat and drink the eucharist (the word means thanks and is allied to blessing, the Hebrew *berakah*) if they thought that with his resurrection the reign had come but not come fully.

If we ask, "Yes, but was there a real last supper like the one recorded?" we put a question that contains a contradiction. What is recorded in the first three gospels and Paul is the *seder* of Christians in four different churches. It resembles the description in Exodus 12 of the Passover *seder*, given as if it were described by the LORD to Moses and Aaron.

As to Jesus' presence in the midst of Christians in bread and cup, the character of Semitic symbol could not have made it more "real" for those who believed in him. The God of Israel is with his people in symbol whenever they remember their deliverance. It is the same with Christians. Their Lord, Jesus, is with them when they eat and drink together. Jesus' followers did something different from their Jewish forebears, however. They took the reality of symbol a step further. They ate bread and drank wine and were convinced that in the very food their Lord was present. It was for them a presence of God.

---

22. Is 25:6, 8

17

The
Teacher of
Renunciation

NOTHING REPORTED OF THE CONDUCT OR TEACHING OF JESUS should lead the Christian church to be nervous about sexuality. A strong position of compassion for female offenders (better, victims) is evident in the quality of Jesus' responses. One can imagine that his followers, in taking him seriously, would favor the monogamous fidelity praised in Genesis 2 over the relaxation provided to wronged or dissatisfied husbands in Deuteronomy 24. As to widespread abstention from sex and parenthood on the basis of Jesus' freedom from family ties, we should not expect it from anything he did or said. He asked the whole world to follow him in his obedience to the Father's will; he was not insistent that anyone imitate him in the details of his lifestyle.

Neither the voluntarily unmarried that Christianity later praised, nor the opponents of sex it dispraised, find their origins in the behavior of Jesus. A reenforcement of Jewish teaching on chastity in thought and deed is to be found in his word on lustful gazes. We can see how some followers who were as absorbed as Jesus was in the preaching of God's reign might have found no time for home and family. But Jesus' opposition to adultery is by no means to be equated with opposition to marital sex.

Two pieces of data need to be examined to give us a complete picture of Jesus' life and words as models for later church teaching on sex. One is his utterance on the renunciation of sex and family for the sake of the new age. The other is the story of his own conception and birth. The latter provided a model of both virginity and motherhood, ideals that have been enormously influential when the two are found together, although motherhood here must be understood in a figurative sense.

Matthew alone provides a saying of Jesus about the preferability of not marrying to doing so. This teaching is a puzzling one to us moderns, like much of what he said. Over the centuries, it has provided the basis for arguments about his meaning, so we should not approach it too confidently. He has just concluded saying that any remarriage by a man who divorces his wife is adulterous. He goes on: "And the man who marries a divorced woman commits adultery."[1] His disciples pick him up on this. Even though he has designated incest (*porneia*) as an exception to his general statement, his disciples check him immediately. The force of his shocking generalization is not lost on them: "If that is the case between man and wife, it is better not to marry."[2] He does not say no to that. If anything, he wades in deeper:

> Not everyone can accept this teaching, only those to whom it is given to do so. Some men are incapable of sexual activity from birth; some have been deliberately made so; and some there are who have freely renounced sex for the sake of God's reign. Let him accept this teaching who can.[3]

This is Jesus' famous "eunuch" saying, for that is the Greek word that occurs three times in Matthew. The translation above goes on the assumption that he is talking about the impotent or sterile and the castrated in order to lead up to his own teaching about the male who voluntarily does not beget children. Such a one

---

1. Mt 19:9; see Mk 10:11-12   2. Mt 19:10   3. Mt 19:12

is to be either a sign of the new age or an agent in bringing it on. Jesus concludes with a word of freedom that might serve as his view of all ascetical practice. Let whoever accepts it do so in the hope that he will be equal to its demands. It is, above all, a matter of personal choice.

Gentiles castrated their captives in an age-old punishment. Jews did not. Those in power castrated the men they put in charge of their women and property. The practice resulted in the use of the word "eunuch" for a king's steward or factotum, even apart from his physical condition. Jesus was not understood by his early followers to be praising the practice of maiming. Later literalists (like a eunuch Justin commends or the popes who created boy sopranos for the Sistine choir) took Jesus to be favoring castration—or so it was said. They were clearly confused as to the figurative quality of Semitic speech. Jesus was rather praising abstention from sex by some with a view to the furtherance of God's reign over all.

Who were the "some"? The teaching occurs in the context of a discussion on marriage, if we can speak of context in a collection of his sayings. The first possibility is that Jesus had in mind the married who were wronged by their partners. The divorced wife or the divorcing husband was a familiar figure in his day. It was often done by simple abandonment. Legal process then as now required submission to the judgment of a court. Many took no chance of losing—either money or the suit. This has led some readers of Matthew to hold that in his eunuch-saying Jesus had in mind only the married and subsequently divorced. He was urging on them continued fidelity despite separation from their partners. Such an interpretation sees Jesus making explicit what had been implicit in another saying that preceded this one: "Therefore, let no man separate what God has joined."[4] He has been quizzed directly on whether he means no remarriage, ever, while the other partner lives— and is saying yes. The terms of expectation of the new age demand it.

A difficulty against this position, which at first seems simple and logical, is that "context" in the gospels means the way the authors chose to group Jesus' sayings. We can never be sure that he

---

4. Mt 19:6

said on the same occasion those statements that are reported together. This is easy to demonstrate since different gospels put the same saying in different contexts, thereby giving them different meanings. We are safer to say that Matthew had in mind a reference to the married than to say that Jesus was confining this teaching to them. The difficulty is compounded because there is no use made of the saying in another gospel.

A better clue is given by another word of Jesus occurring later in the same chapter in Matthew. Here the context is not sex and family life but being rich and having possessions. Peter has said to Jesus: "Here we have put everything aside to follow you. What can we expect from it?"[5] Jesus answers that in the new age, when the son of man takes his seat on a throne of glory, "You who have followed me shall likewise take your places on twelve thrones to judge the twelve tribes of Israel."[6] Then, in a grouping of sayings that Matthew gets from Mark, he has Jesus add:

> Moreover, everyone who has given up home, brothers or sisters, father or mother, wife or children or property for my sake will receive a hundredfold and inherit the life of the final age.[7]

Reporting the same teaching, Mark has Jesus rewarding those who renounce possessions for his sake and the gospel a hundredfold in this age and everlasting life in the age to come.[8]

The question is: Did Jesus ever utter the Matthew saying, and was he as enthusiastic for abstaining from marriage as he seems to have been for putting the demands of family life to one side? They are not, after all, the same thing. The key lies in the imagery of judging the twelve tribes from twelve thrones. Jesus is speaking in figure, and at the same time speaking in earnest. Anyone who takes him with exact literalness, whether in the matter of turning the other cheek, walking a second mile, or leaving one's family, misconstrues him. The last thing he means to do is promulgate a new understanding of the law or the kingdom that is to be followed with literal fidelity.

---

5. Mt 19:27   6. Mt 19:28   7. Mt 19:29
8. See Mk 10:30; Lk (18:29–30) follows Mark but abbreviates the saying

He is a struggler for the life of the spirit; he wants to be followed in the spirit. His several other statements about renouncing goods and human ties add up to one thing: in any conflict between God's demands and human demands, choose God's. How does one know the choices that favor God's reign which, after Jesus' day, came to be understood as fidelity to the gospel? All he says is: You will know. You must choose. No one can choose for you.

Does this make us certain of where Jesus stood on sex and marriage and a life lived without them? Not quite, but it gives us enough to go on. He was a Jew. This means that he stood for a chaste sex life for the unmarried and a faithful one for the married. Jesus could foresee people making a choice like his in lives like his. In helping bring about God's reign, others might have too much to do to take on a marriage partner and a family. Yet no case can be made for his hostility to sex. We know from later history that Greek and gnostic sentiments against material life infected segments of Judaism and Christianity. Sexual activity was so separated from pleasure in both communities that it was rigorously confined to attempts to conceive. There is no evidence from the gospels that Jesus was so infected. By zeal for the kingdom, yes; by revulsion at the claims of life in the body, no. The confusions that arose about sex in the Christian church came after him but not from him.

They may have been influenced, however, by a second aspect of his life, which two of the gospels report. Both Matthew and Luke provide theological prologues, each two chapters long, that draw attention to who Jesus is by spelling out how he came to birth. This kind of tale is familiar from the Bible. It is told in conjunction with Isaac and Moses and Samuel. For the two gospel authors, Jesus' origins were unique because he was unique. Each provided him with a genealogy. Luke's went back to Adam, Matthew's came forward from Abraham. Neither is interested in the exact names provided, since each is doing something more important. They are tracing a divine plan that culminates in this person whose deeds and words they mean to tell.

Both Matthew and Luke attribute the birth of Jesus to the power of God's holy spirit. His conception, like that of the great ones of Israel's history, is more God's doing than humanity's. The two evangelists go further. They call on the biblical tradition that knew Israel as the LORD's bride, hence virginal by definition, and make Jesus' mother, Mary, a virgin at the conception of the child. The symbolism is understandable in light of the conviction that Jesus is the fulfillment of Jewish hopes of all the ages.

But then, all the chaste were virginal at the conception of their first child. Luke hints at more, while Matthew is explicit. The impregnation of this woman, the latter says, is not the doing of Joseph with whom Mary is arranged to be married. This just man, a dreamer like the patriarch whose name he bears, is told in a dream that Mary has conceived and that it is the doing of God's holy spirit. A snatch from Isaiah about a child to become Immanuel, "With us is our God," is cited by Matthew.[9] The mother of the child prophesied may be the prophet's wife. The son she bears would be the one named "Quick Spoils, Speedy Plunder."[10] Or again, it may be King Ahaz's wife and her son Hezekiah. That is not important to Matthew. He is more attracted by that title Immanuel which, so far as we can tell, was not used as the actual name of any boy. If the king were meant, it would be as if a throne name.

Matthew finds biblical support a second time. The Greek translation of Isaiah he is using calls the woman a virgin. The Hebrew had merely called her a young woman. It all fits in perfectly with the virgin symbolism of the fruitful people Israel. That is probably what influenced the translator of the Septuagint Greek Bible to render "young woman" by "virgin" in the first place. It certainly influenced Matthew.

The virgin symbol has influenced the Christian church ever since. It has left its stamp on the church's view of sexuality. Jews, like most of the peoples of the earth, put a high value on virginity as the optimum condition of brides. Christians, probably as the result of the Mary story in Luke, gave virginity an independent existence without reference to subsequent marriage. It is hard to be certain that Matthew and Luke meant to describe Mary as physically virginal in her conception of Jesus. They probably did. But they were more intent on describing her as virginal in another way.

"Virginal in another way" makes moderns guffaw. Even the third- and fourth-century church of Greeks and Romans had trou-

---

9. Is 7:14   10. See Is 8:1-3, 8, 10

ble with it. Their virginity was the physical kind, not the symbolic. Semitic symbols escaped them, once they had given up their own pagan mythology. As a result of the two different outlooks of the Jewish-oriented evangelists and the literalist Greeks and Romans, some students of the gospels hold that while early Luke and Matthew are symbolical, they are not historical. That, they go on to say, is what really matters. They point out that the brothers and sisters of Jesus in the gospels are so evidently his siblings that Mary's ever-virginal status cannot be a fact. Others hold that while Luke and Matthew may be symbolical, they are historical. This, they go on to say, is what really matters. They hold that "brothers" and "sisters" describe nonsiblings in an extended family, and point out that when "brother" or "sister" appears in the New Testament as a description of believers, no such strict construction is put on it.

As we have said, some maintain that the symbolism of the Bible is so much to the fore in the first two chapters of Matthew and Luke that we cannot be certain if they were taking a position on Mary's physical virginal conception. The two authors were sure her virginity was real, but they lived in a world that knew more kinds of real than we do. Their concern was that Mary was virginal as the people Israel, ideally, was, namely, made fruitful by God alone. If Joseph were the physical father of Jesus (although both are clear that he was not), that would have been all right with them. We cannot know, in sum, whether they meant to face the one question that we moderns think is *the* question.

Regarding Christianity and sex, no one can ever know the suffering that single people have endured, and the married, and the divorced, and the lonely, in the name of Jesus' teaching about marriage and divorce, about sex and children. The relief he offered to women oppressed by divorce, which hardly outweighs the suffering, is easier to compute. Can anyone imagine this reconciler, this healer, in the role of patron of the misery that has been multiplied about sexuality in his name?

Careful reflection on what he taught shows that he stood for free renunciation for a purpose, for a season, even perhaps for a lifetime.

As to multiplying human misery regarding marriage or divorce, the blame lies elsewhere. It does not fall on him.

18

The
Respecter of
Women

WHAT DO YOU DO WITH A MAN WHO DOES NOT HAVE ANY sex life? Our culture is embarrassed by him and invents one, or speculates in lively fashion on its absence.

The writers of the four gospels tell us nothing of Jesus' love for any woman. Two of the gospels complicate matters by reporting—or seeming to—that he was conceived and born out of the ordinary course of nature. His total situation was, at the very least, unusual.

This would not have been the case in his adult years if he were a man of India or even ancient Greece. In both places, abstention from all that is passionate is understood. The person who has won control, who has separated himself or herself from the suffering that inevitably accompanies desire, is approved without comment.

Another Indian pattern is the begetting of sons as the proper business of early manhood. That done, and the ordinary civic or business demands attended to, one turns as early as one can to the real business of life: philosophy, contemplation, release from all that binds.

Jesus was born of a Semitic people. Offspring were a means of personal affirmation for male and female alike. They comprised a kind of personal immortality. Sterility was a reproach from God. The ideal state of things for a man in that culture is described in a psalm:

Your wife shall be like a fruitful vine
    in the recesses of your home;
Your children like olive plants
    around your table. . . .
May you see the prosperity of Jerusalem
    all the days of your life;
May you see your children's children.[1]

We cannot be sure that Jesus had not married and then left his home, as some had done before him when struck by the prophetic call. Yet the supposition that he did marry is gratuitous. Mention of a wife or children, if such there were, would be fitting at many points in the gospel narrative. There is none.

The unusual character of such abstention is frequently alleged, not without some hint of infection of the Jewish tradition by a foreign element, whether Persian or Greek. The unmarried few of the Bible are at times catalogued, either to underscore their fewness or to cite precedents for Jesus. The like situations of the Baptizer and of Paul are sometimes adduced, again either exemplarily or by way of deploring an aberration in Judaism before 70 c.e. under outside influence. The foreshortened outlook of one who was an active apocalyptist is also named as a factor. A person convinced that the end is near, it is said, does not prepare for another generation. Still, the answer to the problem of Jesus' unmarried status does not seem to lie in any of these explanations.

---

1. Ps 128:3, 5-6

The meager records of the rabbinic community around Jesus' time tell of a person or two who forewent marriage and parenthood so as to devote himself the more unremittingly to the Torah. Importantly, no wife is mentioned in the case of the rabbis whose names remain to us. The scholars are presumed to have married unless some point is made to the contrary.

As to romantic love, we know almost nothing about it from the biblical or talmudic worlds. There are ample data on the "good wife"; she is a provident householder who is not a scold. Prostitution as a social fact is well documented. So are adultery and lust. The Song of Songs provides us with some chaste erotic poetry, the two being not incompatible in the biblical world. Yet we do not have examples from the ancient literature of "falling in love," or courting, or marrying for love of the woman or man of one's choice. All of those ideas come out of the post-Renaissance period, not from the ancient world. We should not expect to find them in the gospels.

When we read modern descriptions of Jesus' attraction to Mary of Bethany or Mary Magdalene, an attraction he suppressed or sublimated on some higher principle, we can be sure that the magnetism alleged is a product of the imagination of our time. The four gospels describe the mutual respect of Jesus and women, which it is probably correct to call love. That is about the sum of it.

The same lively imagination accounts for contemporary intimations that the fourth evangelist's "disciple whom Jesus loved" was someone he had a homosexual relation with. It is true that this disciple leaned back on Jesus' chest at the last supper, but then it was the one season of the year when Israel reclined to eat. Someone had to be next to him and the fact of who it was, was noted. That unnamed person seems to be the chief apostolic authority for the evangelist John. The mysterious young man who, in Mark's gospel, fled from the garden naked—his linen garment falling to the ground as he got away—is an even less likely candidate for sexual intimacy, since this is clearly a cautionary tale about the fleeing disciples just described. The ancient world knew about the intimacy of men with men but the world of Jewish piety did not countenance it. Jesus was Jewish and he was pious.

The silence of the gospels about his having a wife is the largest piece of evidence we possess. What is to be made of it? The best answer seems to be, neither too much nor too little. The right thing to make of it, in light of all we are told of his concentration on his mission, is that he did not have time for the demands of domestic life. His gypsy existence, the crowds, the never-ending requests for cures saw to that. Simon Peter, it is true, was there for much of it and he is described as a married man. Why not Jesus? We end in ignorance on that score. We can only conclude that if he had had a wife he would have known how to love her.

Family ties have never been a problem for the great ones of religious history. Some were married, some were not. Of many we do not know enough to be sure. The God who raised them up for leadership is not embarrassed by the mystery of sex; humanity may be but divinity is not. The begetting and rearing of children is part of the business of life. It is only a confused human race that rejects it. Whatever settlement Jesus arrived at for himself, he did not reject it.

Isaiah wrote long ago, "As a woman about to give birth writhes and cries out in her pains, so were we in your presence, O LORD."[2] The evangelist John found it easy to illustrate the alternation of human joy and sorrow by accommodating those lines about the mystery of childbearing to Jesus' impending departure: "When a woman is in labor she is sorry that her time has come. When she has borne her child she no longer remembers her pain for joy that a child has been born into the world."[3] The same writer places him in the midst of the hubbub of a wedding at which the wine ran out— not, conceivably, as a result of cautious sipping.[4] If Jesus had been known to be opposed to sex or wine, the story of his providing more wine at the height of wedding festivities would never have been told. We assume from this report that everything that was natural to the human race was natural to him. For himself, he had a work to do. He had to cast a fire of judgment on the earth and be plunged into a baptismal bath of pain. He lived a life of constraint until both were over.[5]

One thing that should be noted is his relative relaxation, for a *hasid*, in the company of women. It would be a mistake to impose later cultural mores on an earlier period, but a first-century situa-

---

2. Is 26:17   3. Jn 16:21   4. See Jn 2:1–11   5. See Lk 12:49–50

tion seems to be hinted at in John's account of Jesus' exchange with a woman of Samaria in a public place. "You are a Jew," she said. "How can you ask me, a Samaritan and a woman, for a drink?"[6] The author reminds the reader that Jews do not use vessels in common with Samaritans, while tactfully omitting mention of any taboo about women. He raises it later by saying:

> His disciples, returning at this point, were surprised that Jesus was speaking with a woman. No one put a question, however, such as "What do you want of him?" or "Why are you talking with her?"[7]

The fact that the woman is described in the story as much-married is scarcely to the point. In the well-known inclination of John to symbolism, this may have been a reference to five of Samaria's previous liaisons, culminating in the current one at the wrong shrine, Mt. Gerizim. But if the woman's life were in fact disordered, that would have fit in well with the kind of company Jesus kept. Luke tells of a woman "known in the town to be a sinner" who made a fuss over Jesus as he ate in the home of a hospitable Pharisee.[8] If her demonstrative behavior and her condition were embarrassing to the host Simon, they were anything but that to the guest Jesus. He not only took her generous attentions to his person in stride, he praised her great love and said it had brought her forgiveness.[9] Puzzled readers have been wondering ever since if Jesus meant to dignify by the word "love" her amours or was only speaking of her solicitude of him; or neither. He does not say. Therein lies a part of his greatness, in the things he does not say.

　　Jesus' best-known act of clemency, perhaps, concerns a woman caught in adultery. There is a certain fittingness in the fact that its status as part of the gospel text is doubtful. The story does not occur in the oldest manuscripts we have of John's gospel. Where it does, it is given as the beginning of the eighth chapter. There are manuscripts that place it after Luke 21:38, where people are listening to Jesus in the temple area just before he is apprehended. Whatever its origins, the narrative was probably inserted

---

6. Jn 4:9   7. Jn 4:27   8. See Lk 7:36–50   9. See Lk 7:47–48

into John's gospel at the point it was because later in the eighth chapter Jesus will say, "You pass judgment according to appearances but I pass judgment on no one,"[10] or later still, "I could say much about you in condemnation, but no, I only tell the world what I have heard from him, the truthful One who sent me."[11]

This is one of the world's classic tales about withholding judgment. As the woman's censorious accusers slink away, one by one, to Jesus' tracing on the ground, he finally straightens up to ask: " 'Woman, where did they all disappear to? Has no one condemned you?' 'No one, sir.' 'Nor do I condemn you. Go. But from now on, avoid this sin.' "[12] The story fits in admirably with the life of one who elevated tolerance of a despised class of women to positive praise:

> I assure you, tax-gatherers and prostitutes are entering the kingdom of God before you. When John came preaching a way of righteousness you put no faith in him, but the tax-gatherers and the prostitutes did believe in him.[13]

The Christian tradition has often been accused of squeamishness about sex. The charge is a strange one, given Jesus' robustness with regard to sexual offenders. It should be noted that in his society, as in so many, women were the easy victims of the lusts of men. Of the latter he has no kind word to say. Indeed, one harsh one is recorded:

> You have heard the commandment, "You shall not commit adultery." What I say to you is: anyone who looks lustfully at a woman has already committed adultery with her in his thoughts.[14]

He does not say "curiously" or "admiringly," not even "brazenly." He is not interested in the involuntary stirrings of passion that characterize all sexual attraction. Jesus goes to the heart of lust, which is desire. "With an eye to having her" might translate his words best. The helplessness of women before men who view them as possessions, ego-supports, or proofs of masculinity is what Jesus attacks.

---

10. Jn 8:15   11. Jn 8:26   12. Jn 8:10–11   13. Mt 21:31–32
14. Mt 5:27–28

Woman the temptress he knows nothing about, though Jewish and Christian literature seems to find her on every page. The gospels tell only of Jesus' concern for woman had, woman used, woman rejected.

> It was also said, "Whenever a man divorces his wife he must give her a decree of divorce." What I say to you is: everyone who divorces his wife—except where there has been incest—forces her to commit adultery. The man who marries a divorced woman likewise commits adultery.[15]

Do we have Jesus' teaching here or that of Matthew? When Mark and Luke report him saying the same thing, the phrase "except in the case of *porneia*" does not appear.[16] This has led to the supposition that *adultery* remains as a justifying cause for divorce in Matthew's church, presumably made up of Christians who were keeping the law of Moses on some terms.[17] Mark is the only one who says "the woman who divorces her husband and marries another commits adultery."[18] This suggests that he is writing for a gentile world where women have such a right.

It is clear that even though the three gospels understood the application differently, they all retained Jesus' teaching. He was accusing his male Jewish forebears of a relaxation in marriage laws that led to gross injustice toward women. His phrase is severe: "Because of your hardheartedness Moses let you divorce your wives."[19] That is a charge delivered to men. But men have been growing weary of women from time immemorial. The consequences for women in Jesus' day were severe. The rejected woman did not "find a job." In the dismissal procedure her survival was literally imperiled.

Jesus puts his argument on a familiar basis in his own religious setting. He cites scripture against scripture, asking why the text in Genesis that says that at marriage two become as one flesh must not prevail. "Therefore, let no man separate what God has joined."[20] This is a hard challenge. Does not the teaching that

---

15. Mt 5:31–32; see 19:9   16. See Mk 10:11; Lk 16:18; *moicheia*=adultery
17. Dt 24:1–4 contains the legislation Jesus is commenting on   18. Mk 10:12
19. Mt 19:8   20. Mt 19:6

goes back to the beginning, he asks, take precedence over what suits the convenience of the male?

Christians like to believe that their teaching prohibiting divorce or allowing it only with difficulty is superior to Jewish teaching. Jews find Christian teaching unrealistic. Even more, they see it as less protective of marriage than the teaching of Leviticus, followed in good conscience, which permits divorce.

Neither side pays close attention to Jesus in the argument. What he was asking was: "Men, what are you making of women in manipulating them without recourse? What are you doing to yourselves?"

To this day, no human culture, religious or otherwise, can be proud of its answer to his challenge.

19

The
Man Who
Died Young

IN THE DISCUSSION OF THE MEALS JESUS ATE, WE HAD TO
come beyond his lifetime and explore early eucharistic practice to
make sense of what the gospels tell us of his final meal. But then,
we have to do that if we are to get at what he probably said about
food, sex, marriage and divorce—anything we can think of. The
problem is the same in getting back to the real Moses, the real
Buddha, the real St. Francis. In all these cases, the person, the
message, and interpretation of the message have all become one by
the time the tradition reaches us. The myth is well formed when we
first encounter the person.

Does this make the person unreal? Not necessarily. It means
that he has become real in the lives of thousands by the time we
first hear of him. This poses a dilemma. Will we decide to learn
wisdom from Moses without getting implicated with the Jewish
people, from the Buddha without discovering the India that made

him, from the poor man of Assisi without Catholicity and medieval romance? People have tried to separate person from tradition in all three cases. The venture has failed.

The situation is similar with Jesus. It is praiseworthy to wish to avoid putting faith in an interpretation and to opt to get to the person. It is at the same time impossible. Persons of so little stature that no myths arise to enfold them are not worth seeking ultimate wisdom from. The essential Confucius, Lao Tzu, and Muhammad can be called anthologies, not men. But what a person must there not have been for this rich lode of wisdom to have been identified as his!

The figure of Jesus stands apart from the others named above by the sheer number of stories that clustered around him. The bulk of Mosaic law is greater, of the Qur'an far greater, if our only standard for remembrance were the attribution of a literature to a person. But Mark brought about a change in ancient writing when he devised the form "gospel." Sayings collections had existed before him. The treasure trove of Hillel-sayings we quoted from was assembled to express all that the Mishnaic period aspired to in the saint and scholar. The pagan sages and wonderworkers of the Christian era, Pythagoras and Apollonius of Tyana, had marvels attributed to them in something resembling modern biographies. Mark put the two types of writing together.

Where he was most successful—or from another viewpoint least—was his account of Jesus' sufferings from his arrest to his death on the cross. Mark provided a lively narrative, capable of stirring up the imagination of the reader beyond anything he could have supposed. The figures of the bullying high priest, the weeping Peter, Barabbas released, and the crowd-pleasing Pilate have become part of the literary tradition of the world. The story has been dramatized often, starting with the practice of different voices reading or singing it aloud in the liturgy, because it is in form a drama. "Passion plays" derive from Mark's passion play and the three versions that came after it.

The trouble is, the gospel writers did more than excite sympathy for Jesus. They also aroused antipathy for his captors and tormentors. If Mark is to be believed, these were mostly Jews. He does not neglect to tell us that the Roman prefect Pilate sentenced him to death, a sentence his soldiers carried out by the Roman-style

torture of crucifixion. It is all very strange. The plotters against
Jesus are identified as the chief priests and the scribes.[1] Those who
arrest him are sent by them and the elders.[2] They hand him over to
Pilate at daybreak. At the Roman hearing the chief priests act as his
accusers.[3] Pilate interrogates him but receives no satisfactory reply.
Then, "aware that it was out of jealousy that the chief priests had
handed him over,"[4] he has him scourged and delivered up to be
crucified.[5]

Mark appears to possess a tradition of individual incidents
that he works into a sequential narrative or passion story, using the
narrative techniques he employs elsewhere. Matthew may add
details from another source, but his account of Jesus' suffering is
basically an edited version of Mark. Luke and John do not depend
on each other, but they seem to have access to the same or similar
sources. At many points these come closer to history than Mark's
sources. "Come closer to history" is a relative term. None of the
four is as interested in what actually happened as he is in how the
events fulfill scripture and what they mean. Their purpose is inter-
pretative. We can even call it theological.

Historically speaking, the charge leveled in Luke by "the
whole assemblage" against Jesus before Pilate was fully actionable
under Roman law: "We found this man subverting our nation, op-
posing the payment of taxes to Caesar, and calling himself the
messiah, a king."[6]

That is a clear expression of three seditious offenses. On the
basis of any one of them, a Roman prefect could have passed a
death sentence with dispatch and not have needed to report the incident to Rome. Failing other evidence, that charge will describe
why Jesus died as much as anything we know.

Some students of the question dismiss the tradition of the
wording of a placard over his head as undependable. It occurs,
however, in all four gospels, even if in a different form in each.
Despite its derisive tone, it hints at an imperial sensitivity to power
in Judea, where the Romans had summarily brought Jewish
kingship to an end two dozen years before. The title, probably

---

1. See Mk 14:1, 10–11   2. See Mk 14:43   3. See Mk 15:3   4. Mk 15:10
5. See Mk 15:15   6. Lk 23:2

written on a gypsum-coated board, read in substance, "Jesus of Nazareth, king of Judea."

Any extended discussion of Jesus' last days would have to be an examination of the history of the traditions that led up to the gospel narratives we possess. That is an interesting study, but this book is about who Jesus was, and the fact that he died, and what followed immediately in the lives of his followers. How we got his story is a story in itself.

He died on a political charge; he died because power feared him. A political sentence means the suspicion of political guilt. As we have pointed out, the record is devoid of overt political utterances by him or even political concern. From the tantalizing clues the gospels supply, all kinds of theorizing have been done about the relation between religious and civil power that led to his end. It is not especially conclusive. The empire got rid of him. The temple priesthood is reported as having had a deep interest in the case.

We do not know the frame of mind in which Jesus faced his death or what construction he put on it. There are three predictions attributed to him in Mark that are remarkably accurate as to detail.[7] They were doubtless prophecies after the event, but they hint at premonitions expressed by him that remained in the minds of the hearers. There is the gospel story of his solitary suffering in prayer on the night he was apprehended. It has too firm a place in the tradition to be dismissed lightly. The elaborations of it in the different gospels should not put us off. All paint a picture of a man who trusts God perfectly but who is in a state of dread of what lies before him. The two do not exclude each other.

We have to go carefully here because the secret colloquies of Jesus with God escaped any recording hand. A band of his friends accompanied him to the Mount of Olives at the conclusion of the supper and a final hymn. It is not a long walk from the plateau the city is built on. In today's Jerusalem you go out an eastern gate of the old city, like St. Stephen's Gate or the southern Dung Gate near the western wall, and make your way downward on a winding macadam road. The ravine you find yourself in is called Kidron, in ancient times the site of a brook. A grove on the farther hillside is

---

7. See Mk 8:31; 9:31; 10:33–34

pointed out as Gethsemane ("olive press"), a plot of land that could have been put to the same use two thousand years ago. A church of the Franciscans on its lower slope houses a rock Jesus is supposed to have prayed on. Despite the impressive formation of the rugged mass, nothing in the gospels leads us to conclude that the site of his prayer can be identified. We are told merely that he "fell on his face,"[8] "fell to the ground,"[9] or "knelt down"[10] to pray. Mark's account of his utterance is repeated essentially by Matthew and Luke: "He kept saying: *Abba* (Father), you have the power to do all things. Take this cup away from me. But let it be as you would have it, not as I.' "[11]

Three disciples are described as having fallen asleep nearby, the Peter, James, and John who enjoyed a special intimacy and were with him on the mountain when he was visibly transformed. Their heaviness in sleep and Jesus' need to rouse them a conventional three times are part of a pattern of desertion and denial by Peter that doubtless had some grounding in fact. Luke alone has Jesus pouring sweat "like drops of blood falling to the ground" and comforted by an angel.[12] All of the first three gospels have Jesus refer to the disciples' trial or testing. It is the word used toward the end of the Our Father for the temptation of the just in the last age.

Jesus' arrest in the garden, his betrayal by Judas, and the identity of his captors and those they represented are told in ways that make it impossible to separate fact from dramatic development. The same is especially true of his appearance before a high priest. The latter is variously described as the current incumbent, Caiaphas (*Qayyiphah*), or his still influential father-in-law Annas (*Ḥanan*). Mark adds to the uncertainty by seeming to have a trial or hearing before the Sanhedrin, the supreme council of Judaism, at night.

There are not sufficient data available on the specifics of Jewish court procedure and Roman justice of that period to know exactly how the proceedings in the gospels compare with either. One derives the clear impression that Jesus was dispatched in haste. The accounts of this haste appear to be reconstructions made from biblical text-fulfillment, a predisposition toward priestly guilt and

---

8. Mt 26:39   9. Mk 14:35   10. Lk 22:41   11. Mk 14:36   12. Lk 22:44

Roman indifference, and some historical reminiscence. The most regrettable feature of the accounts is the appearance given of a Jewish trial and a Roman hearing. In fact, there had to be a Roman trial; there may have been a Jewish hearing.

We mentioned that the charge on which Jesus was brought before Pilate was threefold in Luke. Matthew reports it as a single and blunt: "Jesus was arraigned before the governor, who questioned him: 'Are you the king of Judea?' "[13] This man asks if he were a messianic revolutionary, a breed he was grimly familiar with. Jesus' answer to all such direct questioning, whether put by a civil or a religious functionary, is in every case but one an uninformative "It is you who say so." The exception is Mark, who has him respond to the high priest: "I am." Mark then goes on to use the occasion for his own statement about Jesus as the object of religious faith, a statement he puts on Jesus' lips.

The cryptic non-response of all the other replies, interspersed with Jesus' silence before challenge, leaves the impression of an accused who is uncooperative. Convinced of his innocence, he does not utter a word. The theological constructs that are substituted for genuine testimony help us to know the faith of the early church in Jesus; they do not clarify the historical situation. They leave us mainly with the picture of a Jesus who holds on to life tenaciously. The meaning of drinking the cup if he has to, a phrase attributed to him in the agony in the garden, comes through in the arraignment accounts. Throughout, this man of mercy never loses his grip on a Jewish sense of justice.

The gospels underscore Jesus' Semitic and quite unphilosophical resistance to death—accepting it only as the Father's will—when they say that he uttered a loud cry before yielding up his spirit.

He was a hard man in many ways, not a soft one. Luke's gospel reports a saying of his about the effect he thought he would have that sounds consistent with his other utterances. The tradition had applied to him the verse of a psalm that reads: 'The stone which the builders rejected has become the keystone of the struc-

---

13. Mt 27:11

ture."[14] Originally, the unprepossessing people Israel was intended. Despised by Egypt, Assyria, Babylon, and Persia, it nevertheless had a central place in God's design. The saying of Jesus used uniquely by Luke to comment on the application of this psalm verse to himself is: 'The man who falls on that stone will be smashed to pieces. It will make dust of anyone it falls on."[15]

The story of the crucifixion of Jesus is the ancient story of the death of a good man, an innocent, persecuted Jew. That it should have ended in the popular imagination as a tale of the killing of the founder of one religious group by members of another is tragic. It has nothing to do with that. Any such interpretation would resemble holding it against modern Greeks that Socrates was put to death by Greeks in Athens. In fact, the parallel is not very useful, since it was an occupying power out of sympathy with all Jewish aspirations that put Jesus of Nazareth to death.

The men who wrote the gospels interpreted for their readers what his death meant. Paul carried the process of theological interpretation further. The author of the anonymous Epistle to the Hebrews went furthest of all in theologizing the event. This is rightly called myth-making, the creation of literary structures to convey religious convictions. There is no way to stop it. With a great theme to consider, like a life of integrity snuffed out by forces devoid of such integrity, there are only certain directions the process of interpretation can go in. Among them are enlargement of spirit, life for the many, rescue from alienation.

What other possibilities are there, when it is a matter of appropriating the life of a just man to the life of a believing community? Barabbas and Judas and the women at the cross seem like puny figures here. They are barely able to mirror the dark and light places, the profound faith, the mere, uncomprehending being-there of human hearts. The gospel writers ask them to bear that burden; it is doubtful they can do so.

The mindless tragedy, yet the redeeming possibilities, of Jesus' death can be an instructive lesson to all humanity. It can, that is, provided no one takes the dramatic development of the four

---

14. Ps 118:22   15. Lk 20:18

gospels to be an exercise in history. They are not that, but theology. Theology tries to understand how God is at work in the midst of humanity.

Jesus was a person of candor, aggression, obedience, trust. Above all, he was concerned for the abandoned who had no representation in high councils. He was destroyed at the hands of suspicion, bluff, self-interest, fear. It does not matter whose. The deep desire to remain in power met a man who said, "No." That man had to die.

Medieval Christian piety concentrated on the physical sufferings of Jesus. The modern age, characteristically, has turned to his mental anguish. Neither seems to be at the center of his death. What matters centrally is the age-old biblical problem of the death of the just at the hands of the wicked. Why do the good die violently? Why must they be destroyed precisely because they are truthful and just? What does God have against the Jews, his "chosen," that he lets them die this way? Jeremiah raised the question in his own person as the target of malevolence. So did the authors of many psalms and the anonymous poet we call the Second Isaiah. They all concluded in mystification. They knew only this, that if they were to keep their honor and their trust in God they had to die.

The answer of Jesus to death was the answer of Job to life. There is God and God will vindicate the just.

How, no one knows.

20

The
Man Raised
from the Dead

MOST WRITING ABOUT THE RESURRECTION OF JESUS IS ARGU-
mentative. It wishes to establish that it could have happened or
could not have happened. Sometimes it goes on the assumption
that, since it happened, the human race must do something about
it. The authors of the gospels and Saint Paul did not go about it
that way. The book of Acts does.

Reading what the gospels have to say about Jesus' risen life
—and they nowhere describe him as rising, only as risen—is instructive. The tone is laconic, direct, matter-of-fact. You find
words like "perplexed," "frightened," and "amazed" to describe the
reactions of the early experiencers of his presence as risen, but that
is not the general tenor of the accounts. They are concerned with an
ordinary, dialogue-type encounter with him, at least those that
come after the accounts of the earliest appearances to certain
women near his tomb on the first day of the week.

One wonders how it came about that the most unusual happenings in this sequence are reported in a tone we might employ to tell of a trip to a nearby town. The stories of the treatment of Jesus by his captors and his progress to the place of execution are much more dramatically recounted. The accounts of his appearing behind (through?) locked doors, or telling certain women that his friends should go to Galilee where he would meet them, are models of sobriety. After he is risen, he becomes as if an occasional visitor from another sphere.

The key to the narratives is that he is a visitor not from another sphere but from another age, a new eon that has begun with him.

It is impossible to understand what Jesus' rising from the dead is about if we think of it as the resuscitation of a dead man. He is not described as starting life over again. He did not mythically represent new vegetation after the rains of winter are over, or human life perpetually coming forth from the dark womb of earth. He was, for the Jews who first believed in him, the "first-fruits" of a harvest of all the dead. If you had the faith of the Pharisees, his appearance would have startled you, but it would not have surprised you. You would have been stunned chiefly that he was *alone.* That he was risen in the body was something that ultimately you could cope with.

It seems strange, at this distance of years, to try to re-create a world we have such sparse information about. We cannot reconstruct ancient Jewish religious thought and make it ours. We can save ourselves a lot of headaches, though, if we realize how much preparedness there was in those times for the notion of being raised from the dead.

Preachers like to say of Jesus' disciples: "Their hopes were dashed. They were fugitives because of their association with him. They were not likely, after forty hours of cowed subjection, to have come up with a tale of victory over death." That may be true. It probably is true. But it is not the point. The point is what his disciples were mentally ready for, given the initial shock of encounter. We of the Western hemisphere are prepared for reports about technological possibilities that the Papuan bushman cannot take in. An Iowa farm couple can absorb readily what two prisoners of Second Avenue could not make sense of. In the same way, a person's being

raised from the dead as the beginning— however meager—of the
age that was to come was an idea that all the witnesses of Jesus'
risen state could handle. They may not have been expecting it that
morning, but seeing him they did not shout "Ghost!" or have visions of Bela Lugosi. They had had a couple of centuries of preparation for the notion—quite strange to us—of the vindication of the
just through living again in the flesh. Since the Maccabean revolt
there had been renewed faith in what God would do for those faithful to him who had died at the hands of gentile tyrants.

This is not to say that Jesus' rising from the dead was
dreamed up because the whole culture was ready for it. It is an attempt to situate it in the religious thought of the times. Any Jews
who saw him, or thought they did, would immediately begin to
think different thoughts from ours. We would say, "I'm seeing
things!" And, in fact, Luke, who does not seem to know Jewish
thought very well, has the disciples labeling the women's tale
"nonsense."[1] After an initial shock no less than ours, Pharisaic Jews
like Peter and James would think, "God's reign has begun! But
where are the others?"

It is a mistake, in a sense, to keep saying "rising" and "risen"
about Jesus, because the earliest accounts in the gospels are all in
the passive voice: "He was raised" or "has been raised."[2] This
betrays the conviction of the writers that the God of Israel was the
chief actor. Probably the later view of Christians concerning Jesus'
power, or his coming forth from the tomb as proving something
about *him*, accounted for the translations of the verb as active. But
for the evangelists, the deed proved something about *God*. He had
not forgotten his servant Jesus, the one he had sent "with miracles,
wonders, and signs as his credentials. . . . God freed him from
death's bitter pangs and raised him up again, for it was impossible
that death should keep its hold on him."[3]

The gospel accounts of Jesus' being raised have as their focus
a rock tomb. The Jews buried that way. You can see in Jerusalem to
this day the tombs of a king and queen of Adiabene in Mesopotamia (modern Iraq) who were converts to Judaism before Jesus'

---

1. See Lk 24:11, 37-39   2. See Mk 16:6, Mt 28:7; 1 Cor 15:4
3. Acts 2:22, 24

time. There is, first, a kind of antechamber you stoop low to enter. Mourners sat there. Then, in the inner chamber, the corpses themselves were placed. In those tombs on the Nablus Road (in Hebrew, *Derek Shechem*) in East Jerusalem there are some round, millstone-shaped slabs that covered the doors of the tombs. Mark writes of three women who went to the burial place, found the stone rolled back, and the "place where they laid him," empty.[4] The details of the story are different in the other gospels, but the central matter around which the various stories cluster is the same: the tomb is empty. In his second book, a story of the early Christians, Luke makes a big thing of the fact that anyone can examine David's grave.[5] Jesus' tomb, presumably, is not being venerated by his followers.

This presents us with the question: Did an empty tomb give rise to the resurrection story or was there a resurrection that gave rise to the story of the empty tomb? In which direction did matters go?

Matthew moved in circles where the story was still current, fifty years later, that Jesus' disciples stole the body.[6] He tells the counter-story that some of the chief priests and elders, having suspected that such a theft might take place, bribed the soldiers to say: "His disciples came during the night and stole him while we were asleep."[7] This account is so specific that one can hear in it echoes of debates about the resurrection in the 80s. By that time it is being argued like the story of a modern crime.

It would help if we could say, without ifs or ands, that the earliest traditions we have on Jesus risen spoke first of an empty tomb and then of his appearance to certain witnesses. Unfortunately, the earliest tradition of all is not clear on the point.

The first written summary of the tradition occurs in a letter of Paul some twenty-five years after the event described. Mark does not write until another fifteen or twenty years have passed. Paul was not in Jerusalem in the year 30 that we can be sure of, and had no interest in the Jesus question in any case. He passes along the tradition the way it reached him, no doubt from the com-

---

4. See Mk 16:1–6; Lk 24:3; Jn 20:2   5. Acts 2:29   6. See Mt 28:15
7. Mt 28:13; see 27:62–66

munities of Damascus and Antioch in the years when he first joined the Christian movement. When was that? Guesswork, not entirely without foundation, would put that a few years, at the most five, after the crucifixion.

Paul wrote:

> I handed on to you first of all what I myself received, that Christ died for our sins in accordance with the scriptures; that he was buried and, in accordance with the scriptures, was raised on the third day; that he was seen by Cephas, then by the twelve. After that he was seen by five hundred brothers at once, most of whom are still alive, although some have fallen asleep. Next he was seen by James; then by all the apostles. Last of all he was seen by me, as one born out of the normal course.[8]

That is a fragment of what we would nowadays call a creed. It is not a mere catalogue of events but an interpretation of them as well. Christ did not just die, he "died for our sins." More than that, he died and was raised up just as the Bible had said he would be, in the sense understood by those who believed in him. The creed is sufficiently interested in the facts that it ticks them off without elaborating on them at any length. That is the big difference between the churches of Paul and those from which the gospel writers came. The latter were more Palestinian in their approach to things and capitalized on their knowledge, or that of their sources, of the terrain. Paul had no information that he wished to share about the details of Jesus' career. The gospel writers have sufficient information to work the details up into a narrative. We would be much better off if we had from Paul a life of Jesus in the same form, short and schematic, as the list of his appearances in the risen state.

There are two or three important differences between Paul's list and the earliest gospel accounts. He reports on no women witnesses. This is not strange when you consider that their testimony was not accepted in Jewish law courts. The omission should not be attributed to Paul's male chauvinism but to the mentality of the times. Moreover, he does not feature an empty tomb. The phrase

---

8. 1 Cor 15:3–8

"was buried" probably went into the early creed to make the point that Jesus was really dead and did not just seem to be. (It can also be argued that a tomb, once filled and later empty, is being spoken of implicitly here.) Lastly, note that Paul who saw the risen Jesus years later puts himself on the list of those especially accredited witnesses. This means that for him the resurrection was not a question of Jesus' remaining on the earth for forty days, which is the way Luke tells it,[9] or visiting from heaven. It was a personal experience of the Jesus who had put the conditions of this age behind him and had already begun to live the life of the new age.

The way we are going about this makes it sound as though the stories about the young men or angels at the tomb,[10] or Jesus' being clung to by Mary Magdalene,[11] or the disclosure he made of himself to two disciples in the breaking of bread[12] are not important. They are not unimportant but they bear the marks of later elaboration on the central event they underscore. It seems from the stories that Jesus did appear to women before being seen by anyone else, but apart from the Magdalene their exact identity is obscure. A tradition of appearances at meals may also have a basis in fact. The later faith of Christians in the presence of Jesus at a meal, however, tends to put this matter in question.

His giving the gift of the spirit, which was the same as the power to forgive, is not in the same category. Understandably, much that the early Christians believed and did, such as mutual forgiveness as a community, was traced to what took place in the "resurrection appearances." Jesus was put to death in the midst of much unfinished business. More importantly, as now fully God-invested (that is, by "spirit"), he was able to give the gift of spirit.

It is hard to write about the risenness of Jesus. We know from the gospels the traditions that grew around the fact that he was raised up. Of the fact itself we know little: only that whatever happened was powerful enough to create the tradition.

What right have we to call it a fact? That word is not entirely satisfactory, but some word is needed to describe what the many witnesses said they experienced.

---

9. See Acts 1:3   10. See Mt 28:2; Mk 16:5; Lk 24:4; Jn 20:12
11. See Jn 20:17   12. See Lk 24:30-31

In the last two hundred years, with the rise of the modern critical sense of history, the resurrection has been viewed in terms of mass hallucination, of myths of dying and rising gods, even of the development within the community of the Genesis story of Joseph, who was left by his brothers in a cistern that Reuben discovered empty. An approach taken by some theologians over the last fifty years has been to say that it is not primarily a story of Jesus' being raised but of people's faith in what God can do for them. If they believe that God can help them face death and overcome it by not fearing it, they have the resurrection faith that Paul and John are inviting them to.

The resurrection story is by all means about the religious response of people to Jesus Christ. It is not just about something marvelous that happened to him. Still, it is clear that the writers would say that you had missed their meaning entirely if you told them that they had reported on what happened to them but not on what happened to him.

Something happened to him. We are at a loss to describe it on its own terms because they are not the terms of ordinary existence. We are wisest to fall back on the way the New Testament puts it: "He has been raised up. He is not here."[13]

"Here" is not merely a plot of earth or a newly hewn rock tomb, though it is at least that. "Here" is where humanity is: in this age, in history. Jesus, for those who were the first to believe in him, was elsewhere. He was at the border between this age and the next. He had already begun to live the life he himself described:

> You are badly misled, because you fail to understand the scriptures or the power of God. When people rise from the dead . . . they live like the angels in heaven. . . . Have you not read in the book of Moses, in the passage about the burning bush, how God told him, "I am the God of Abraham, the God of Isaac, the God of Jacob"? He is the God of the living, not of the dead.[14]

Call it mythical if you will. That passage from Mark is a fair description of the lively faith in the resurrection that Jesus shared

---

13. Mt 28:6   14. Mk 12:24-27

with the progressive Pharisees of his time but not the conservative Sadducees.

With the destruction of Jerusalem in the year 70, a whole Jewish way of life died. A new one was reborn. More accurately, two new ones. An abyss lay between what had been thought and believed before and the two new ways of thought. It would be somewhat like the shape of the new world if Hitler, God forbid, had won. We cannot guess its outlines, but there would have been at the very least no state of Israel and no resurgence of Jewish life around the globe such as we have witnessed. The tragedy of the Nazi holocaust led to a renewed and reinvigorated Judaism. The destruction of Jerusalem led to an equally vigorous rebirth. What happened after the tragedy of the year 70 was the coming to birth of Israel anew and a tradition springing from it, Christianity. If the Qumrân sect had survived beyond 135, there would have been a third tradition, tiny as it was.

The Israel of New Testament times—the Judaism of today— had no reason to keep alive its faith in the resurrection of the dead through belief in the resurrection of Jesus. He did not become an object of faith for that community.

The offspring of Israel that kept the Pharisee notion of resurrection alive by means of faith in Jesus stopped being Jewish sharply after the year 135.

The net result is a claim that Jesus was raised from the dead made by gentiles who can barely comprehend the Jewish import of what they are saying. They never had the background of the postexilic, Pharisee development. They are innocent of the reality of Jewishness.

Yet they accept the biblical books in their entirety as God-inspired. They believe in the Hebrew revelation. They say they are impelled to do so by their faith in Jesus Christ risen from the dead, a mystery based solidly on Jewish eon-thought.

21

The
Man Believed In

WHO IS JESUS OF NAZARETH TO THE PEOPLE OF OUR AGE? That is the question we started with. We hear about him all the time. You cannot not hear about him. Some of our contemporaries pray in his name and make him the center of their religious lives. Many disregard him. He is a curse or a casual exclamation on the lips of many he means nothing to.

What does a person have to do to end up a curse? No one says "Socrates!" or "Julius Caesar!" to emphasize a point nowadays. Even when people did, they were using substitute names. The subject of a curse or an oath has to be thought sacred somehow if it is to qualify as blasphemy. The Italians still say "Per bacco!" "By Bacchus," and the upper-class English "By Jove!" the short form of Jupiter. Both are ways to say "By God" without saying it. "Gee whiz" and "Cripes" side-step the name and title of Jesus, but there isn't much side-stepping any more. When a person says "Jesus!" with studied casualness, it is meant to be a blasphemy or the effect is lost.

Jesus' name is a conscious blasphemy in our culture, with or without the title "Christ." That says something about widespread belief in him as a divine being, even though many who use the expletive have no such faith. Jesus has to do as their deity because they do not have another.

We have been looking in these pages into who Jesus was in his lifetime. He was not a priest, the most sacred office in the life of his people, even though Luke claimed that his mother was related to a priest named Zechariah through his wife Elizabeth. Jesus was a layman. He respected temple worship and took part in it. But why did the author of the Epistle to the Hebrews make him not only a priest but the great high priest, when in fact he was a Jewish layman?

To find the answer to that question we have to understand the mentality of the two hundred years before Jesus' lifetime. Jewish kingship was at a very low ebb from about the year 150 onward, and so was priesthood. There were nostalgic dreams of how splendid things had been in David's day, but in fact the monarchy had fallen on hard times. The Hasmonean kings—and one queen— who descended from Judah the Maccabee and his sons were not very much. They captured the high priesthood and were priest-kings for a while. This consolidation of power was good for neither politics nor piety.

In Jesus' day, Herod the Great, a king of the Jews of gentile (Idumean) blood, had not been dead long. The bitter memory of him remained strong, however, in the popular mind. In the division of his power by the Romans among three of his sons, when Jesus was ten or twelve, the high priesthood became something that the Romans manipulated. Things got so bad at one point that the empire kept custody of the key to the place where the richly worked high-priestly vestments were kept. The Roman prefects controlled the freedom of men like Annas and Caiaphas to celebrate on feasts like the Day of Atonement. The climax of all these woes came not with Jesus' death, which did not create a ripple in Jewish history, but when a Jewish uprising was mounted in the year 67. The Romans succeeded in crushing it three years later. They sacked the city, destroyed the temple, and left Jewish pride in ashes—for the moment.

No wonder then that the early Christians, all of whom were Jews, dreamed dreams in the images of the past two hundred years of hope: a restored monarchy, a renewed priesthood, an age of prophecy fulfilled. With Jesus' resurrection from the dead, he became the inheritor of every high title the Bible had ever contained.

We have already spoken of the complex relation between Jesus and the office of king (messiah). His steps seem to have been dogged by popular efforts to implicate him with this title, whether as a political reality or a symbolic one. His entry into Jerusalem for his last Passover was the occasion of a wild demonstration in his favor. Such was the mood of a populace desperate for enlightened leadership. The enthusiasm of the many who had seen his works or heard his teaching is understandable.

Pilgrims were met at the edges of the city as they came in from every direction. One of the psalms contains a dialogue between the pious pilgrim who sought entry to Jerusalem ("Open to me the gates of justice;/I will enter them and give thanks to the LORD") and those who admitted him ("This is the day the LORD has made;/let us be glad and rejoice in it"). Toward the end of the psalm the pilgrims already at the feast said to the new arrival:

Blessed is he who comes in the name of the LORD;
  we bless you from the house of the LORD.
The LORD is God and he has given us light.
Join in procession with leafy boughs
  up to the horns of the altar.[1]

The leafy boughs were the branch of palm intertwined with myrtle and willow and another sheaf made of citron branches.

Mark paints a picture of a wild reception on Jesus' behalf that uses the psalm verse just quoted. It is interspersed with a cry that means in Aramaic, "Save, we pray!"

Hosanna!
Blessed is he who comes in the name of the LORD!
Blessed is the reign of our father David to come!
Hosanna in the highest![2]

---

1. Ps 118:26–27   2. Mk 11:9–10

Mark describes a set of mysterious and elaborate directions by
Jesus to procure for his entry into the city an ass's colt that has
never been ridden. Clearly he is having "the Master" act out a verse
from an oracular poem in Zechariah about the meekness of Judah
in contrast with the chariot, horse, and warrior's bow of the collaborationist northern kingdom:

> Rejoice heartily, O daughter of Zion,
>   shout for joy, O daughter Jerusalem!
> See, your king shall come to you;
>   a just savior is he,
> Meek, and riding on an ass,
>   on a colt, the foal of an ass.[3]

Jesus, the "king" of Mark's theological construction, does
not seem very cooperative with his own image when later a companion lunges with his sword at the moment of arrest and cuts off
an ear of one of the apprehenders. Matthew writes:

> "Put back your sword where it belongs. Those who use the
> sword are sooner or later destroyed by it. Do you not suppose
> I can call on my Father to provide at a moment's notice more
> than twelve legions of angels?"[4]

Here as in so many cases it is impossible to discern whether Jesus or
the writer of the gospel is the speaker. But the disinterest of the captive Jesus in that kind of power is fully in character with his other
utterances. His attitude is spelled out in words that bear the
familiar stamp of John's poetry:

> "My kingdom does not belong to this world.
> If my kingdom were of this world,
> my subjects would be fighting
> to save me from being handed over. . . .
> As it is, my kingdom is not here."[5]

We have here the lines of the struggle in which the living
Jesus resists kingship but loses out to his believing followers after he
has left them. They mean to have him as the central figure in the

---

3. Zech 9:9   4. Mt 26:52–53   5. Jn 18:36

"reign of our father David to come." He becomes "both Lord and Messiah, this Jesus whom you crucified,"[6] in the preaching of the early church.

He was made, in Christian faith, not only the monarch in the restored kingdom of the last age, but also the high priest in a liturgy that was begun on the cross "once for all" rather than in Jerusalem's temple. His mediation as high priest continues forever behind the veil of the heavens. In the Epistle to the Hebrews no inkling is given that the temple is destroyed, any more than you can learn this from a reading of the Mishnaic tractate *Pesaḥim* in its description of how the Passover slaughter of beasts is carried out. The Christian author of Hebrews has a set of principles of interpretation not unlike those of Qumrân. He sees the yearly drama of Yom Kippur fulfilled in Jesus. That was the day the high priest entered the Holy of Holies alone, sprinkling blood in the chamber to atone for his sins and those of the people. This was an important reinterpretation to a people that had lost its sole sanctuary, however much it may lack significance to us.

Jesus never mentioned himself in terms of priesthood or sacrifice. Yet these two titles, messiah (or king) and priest, were attributed to him symbolically after his death, despite the fact that realistically both were inconceivable in his lifetime. Again we ask how it was possible. Belief in his resurrection made the difference. This unique occurrence caused Jewish believers in it to attach every possible Jewish title to him. He was son of David, messiah, king. He was the Isaian servant of the LORD who had to suffer.[7] He was the high priest of the "new covenant" of Jeremiah.[8]

Of his priesthood Hebrews has this to say:

> One does not take this honor on his own initiative, but only when called by God as Aaron was. Even Christ did not glorify himself with the office of high priest; he received it from the one who said to him, "You are my son; today I have begotten you."[9]

Notice that the title "Christ" is used almost as if it were a proper name. That is what happened to the Jewish title messiah. When the

---

6. Acts 2:36   7. See Is 42:1–13; 49:1–7; 50:4–9; 52:13—53:12
8. See Jer 31:31   9. Heb 5:5

early Greek-speaking believers in Jesus translated it into Greek as
christos, they in effect changed its meaning. It now meant, not a
king of the Jewish people, but the one who had been anointed by
God as Lord of all.

To these designations of Jesus—say by the year 90 or whenever the first three gospels were completed—there were added the
titles "son of God" in a Greek sense, and "savior." A "son of God,"
as has been pointed out, was to the Jewish ear either the king or any
pious Jew. "Saviors" or "redeemers" the Jews did not have, except
for God himself. But the church was becoming increasingly gentile
in membership by the year 90. Hence, Greek titles came to the fore,
while Jewish ones like "servant of the LORD," "son of man," and
"messiah" receded. In all of these conceptions Jesus was a Jewish
holy man and teacher, not a "second divine being." There could be
no such thing for these staunch monotheists. But they had the per-
sistent problem of who, exactly, this man was, now in glory at
God's right hand.

That was the problem the Christians were facing as they
multiplied titles for Jesus, especially those that connoted divinity in
the Greek world, as many of them did. Was he not threatened with
separation from his real existence as a wandering teacher, a pleader
for the reform of human hearts, by this activity of a community of
faith in him? There was a certain danger here. His followers did not
have the language to avoid it completely.

Meantime, Saint Paul's presentation of Jesus was exclusively
that of the crucified and risen Christ, a Lord who is set over his
"body," whom God associates with himself in the salvation of the
human race.

Mark and the others, in particular Matthew and Luke,
wrote gospels to ensure that people would not forget his teaching.
They stressed his wonders because of their faith in him, but they retained and edited his words. John puts his wonders in perspective
as "signs." There is a passage in the Epistle to the Hebrews which,
in a sense, preserves the real Jesus of Nazareth best of all:

> In the days when he was in the flesh, he offered prayers and
> supplications with loud cries and tears to God, who was able
> to save him from death, and he was heard because of his

reverence. Son though he was, he learned obedience from what he suffered.[10]

This brief sketch of who he was in his lifetime has all the needed elements.

At this distance we may be prone to regret the change that the person of Jesus underwent at the hands of those who believed in him. But this is unrealistic. Who can prescribe what a company of pious Jews should have made out of one of their number who was raised from the dead? They, after all, had a lively faith in the coming of the new age. We do not. They believed that the only meaning he had was to be found in the view they had of God's action. The titles they had ready to hand from their Bible in Greek translation (which the mission to gentiles required) meant everything to them. We would be foolish to complain about the religious presuppositions of another age. Our task is to make some sense out of the same Jesus in our categories.

The Greek religious world is often faulted as if it had done irreparable damage to the simple Jewish saint Jesus. That, again, is easy to do if you do not like Greek ways or if you are sure that that is all he was, a Jewish saint. The realities in the case were that, after the gentile Jewish proselytes who were the bulk of Paul's converts, a Greek pagan world began to show a tremendous interest in the God of Israel through this Jew it could identify with. Naturally, the pagans heard everything that was said about him in *their* way. They could not possibly have had the Hebrew experience. They were too busy having had the Greek, the Phrygian, the Roman experience. The remarkable thing was how Jewish the Christian preachers managed to make these hearers, through presenting Jesus not in splended isolation but in the context of the entire history of his people. They required a thoroughgoing knowledge of the Jewish scriptures. The newly baptized had to become culturally as if they were Jews—though Paul's struggle to keep them from circumcision and the whole yoke of the law is well known. In Jesus, the history of the Jewish people exploded on the Graeco-Roman scene as it had not previously done in the widespread proselyte movement.

---

10. Heb 5:7–8

Religions that go wandering get into trouble. Religions that stay at home likewise get into trouble. Jesus' message was calculated to get all religions into trouble, whether they remained ethnic, branched out, stayed at home, or "got civilized" (the term is a Greek provincialism).

Jesus had something to say to everybody. If the hearer listened carefully, his teaching should not have confirmed the prejudices—read, the religious presuppositions—of anybody. Needless to say, it did. A gentile church came to think his teaching proved the Jews wrong in religion.

But that is scarcely what his person or his teaching was about.

22

The
Jesus of Paul

AN OLD JOKE SAYS, "LOVED HIM. HATED HER." MILLIONS
have said, "Love Jesus. Hate Paul," and it is no joke.

There are all sorts of reasons to be against Saint Paul. He is
too complicated. He does not think women equal to men. He is
dogmatic. Most of all, he invented a new religion called Christianity that worshipped Jesus as God. As part of going in this new
direction, he turned his back on the Judaism of his youth.

These points of view, which for many are convictions,
deserve examination.

Paul did not know Jesus in his lifetime. He not only did not
write a gospel about him, he paid no attention to the facts of his life
except for the last few days. He did transmit a few of his teachings
in wording other than that of the gospels. Paul claimed to have had
a special revelation of Jesus at a time when he was persecuting his
followers. This revelation made him a convert. The singleminded-
ness of converts that sometimes borders on fanaticism is famous.

Aside from what Paul may have learned from the appearance of the risen Jesus to him, he was formed in his discipleship by the churches of Damascus and Antioch. He himself was from Tarsus, like Antioch, in modern Turkey. To reach it you go northwest from Antioch through a mountain pass called the Cilician Gates onto the Asia Minor peninsula. This makes Paul a diaspora Jew, a class highly suspect in Judea.

Paul had a biographer in the person of the author of Luke's gospel and the book of Acts, who worked from sources. This author admired Paul but probably never met him. Paul is the only writer represented in the collection of Christian Scriptures who speaks for himself; the rest of the writings are largely pseudonymous. We have seven letters that he surely wrote and others that were written either by him or disciples who knew his thought. His first extant letter was composed about the year 50, the last one, six or seven years later. Most are lively pieces of correspondence to groups of people he knew. One was written to the Christian community at Rome before he had been there. Only one is to an individual, a wealthy Christian named Philemon whose runaway slave had become a Christian, but even this one asks for community promulgation. Paul tried to put the two men on a basis of equality through their faith in Jesus Christ.

That conviction of equality might stand as his considered view of what it meant to believe in the teacher of Nazareth, as it occurs in another epistle:

All of you are offspring of God because of your faith in Christ Jesus. All of you who have been baptized into Christ have clothed yourselves in him. There does not exist among you Jew or Greek, slave or freeman, male or female. All are one in Christ Jesus.[1]

He also thinks that the internal reconciliation of all humanity and of humanity to God is possible through his fellow Jew Jesus:

He died for all so that those who live might live no longer for themselves but for him who for their sakes died and was raised up. Because of this we no longer look in terms of mere

---

1. Gal 3:26–28

human judgment on anyone. If at one time we so regarded Christ, we no longer know him by this standard. This means that if anyone is in Christ, he is a new creation. The old order has passed away; now all is new. All this has been done by God, who has reconciled us to himself through Christ and has given us the ministry of reconciliation. I mean that God, in Christ, was reconciling the world to himself, not counting people's transgressions against them, and that he has entrusted the message of reconciliation to us.[2]

This overarching view of the possible meaning of Jesus to the human race is applauded by some readers of Paul and deplored by others. Paul at least makes clear what he is up to.

He does not view the words or deeds of Jesus as he once did when Jesus was "flesh," that is, in the former age. He is interested in him only as "spirit," meaning Jesus as someone grasped *totally* by God's spirit in being raised from the dead. Christ the first-fruits of the new age commands all of Paul's attention. The Jesus who "became sin for us,"[3] while he was utterly praiseworthy in having done so, detains Paul only insofar as he is the means to become God's "righteousness" for us. When the fiery little teacher wishes to cite a model for personal conduct, he does not point to Jesus but to himself! It is as if he, Paul, is living proof of the things that are possible to one who believes in Christ. He seems to avoid adopting Jesus as he was before his resurrection as a standard, lest, in Jesus' voluntary association with sinful humanity, he get in the way of the "Christ our righteousness" who succeeded him.

How did Paul come to think the way he did? The narrative, the anecdote is, after all, the usual type of Jewish teaching. Paul either possesses no fund of stories about Jesus or consciously chooses to go another route. The latter may be the case. We are handicapped in our discussion by our ignorance of the rabbinic patterns of argument of the time; no other letters survive from the pens of contemporary rabbis. In fact, we are up against the sparsity of Jewish writing in all fields. Josephus retold the Bible in the first ten books of his Antiquities of the Jews, and went on to write a contemporary military history of his people. Philo in Alexandria re-

---

2. 2 Cor 5:15–19   3. 2 Cor 5:21

counted Jewish convictions in the manner of a philosopher. But as to patterns of sustained rabbinic argumentation that are indisputably from that time, we possess only Paul's letters. What we have from the rabbis comes from the years 70-200 and those writings are anthologies of opinion on disputed fine points. Paul was arguing a case different from that espoused by any rabbi whose utterances survive even fragmentarily. This makes him far from typical. The trouble is, the central figure of Jewish history for Paul was far from typical. As regards method of argument, we do not know whether Paul was typical of his time or not. As to substance, he certainly was not.

He writes frequently that he is under a compulsion to proclaim the message about Jesus arising from a call from God. Thus, he speaks of

> the gospel concerning his son, who was descended from David according to the flesh but was made son of God in power according to the spirit of holiness, by his resurrection from the dead: Jesus Christ our Lord.[4]

Paul is not only not interested in Jesus as he was in life, but not interested in him in isolation in the present. Christ has meaning for him solely in relation to the faith and life of others:

> The God I worship by preaching the gospel of his son will bear witness that I constantly mention you in prayer. . . . What I wish is that we may be mutually encouraged by our common faith.[5]

He thinks of the gospel as "the power of God leading everyone who believes in it to salvation, the Jew first, then the Greek."[6] This priority of Jew over Greek in a calling to the new life that the gospel holds out is a constant with Paul. He can affirm it while saying in the same breath that there is no favoritism with God.[7] It is not an ethnic matter for him, nor is it based on his fellow-Jewishness with Jesus; it is simply a matter of God's ancient promise that God must be faithful to.

---

4. Rom 1:3-4   5. Rom 1:9, 12   6. Rom 1:16   7. See Rom 2:9-11

Paul, like Jesus and the prophets, has a very high standard of conduct for the Jew. He is not satisfied with religious signs like circumcision or claims for the superiority of the law.[8] Where he seems to depart from the teaching of Jesus is in having an equal interest in the Jew and the non-Jew. This difference should not be minimized. Jesus can nowhere be shown to have wished his teaching to reach the gentiles, not to speak of every gentile in the world, except through the renewal of Israel. This people was meant to be a light to the gentiles. The "missionary command" to go to all nations, found on Jesus' lips in Matthew's gospel, is Matthew's conviction rather than Jesus' utterance.

The gospels tell of Jesus' brief forays to Sidon and Tyre on the Phoenician coast and the Ten Cities region across the Jordan, both of them gentile territory. But nothing much is made of it beyond some reported cures and conversations with the local inhabitants. Some have even concluded that, in Jesus' hope, the onset of the new age was so imminent that any transmission of his message beyond the confines of the Jewish people would have been needless. We are convinced that no such case can be made from the apocalyptic language of Jesus that was commonly in use. Paul did, however, go far beyond Jesus in working out a rationale for proclaiming the "good news about Christ" to the gentile world.

This is part of a much larger matter. Jesus proposed to his hearers that God's reign, an idea already familiar to them, was near at hand. He asked for repentance for sin and trust in God, as John the Baptizer had done before him. He nowhere asked for faith in his person as someone the life of the new age would be transmitted through. This is true even though the gospel according to John has him asking for it on every page. Jesus had some strong convictions about his own significance as a prophet, but he referred everything to God.

From the moment his being raised from the dead struck home with his followers, however, they referred everything to God through him. There are many echoes of this in the gospels, which are a literature of retrospect.

---

8. See Rom 2:17–29

Paul followed the lead of those teachers in Antioch who had preceded him. Like the sermons attributed to Peter in the first days of the Jerusalem community, his epistles asked for faith in God through Jesus Christ. He worked out a number of profound patterns and arguments of his own in this regard, but he joined a community of believers that was already doing the same. He by no means invented the notion.

The rabbi of Tarsus may have a lot to answer for, but he cannot be charged with having made of Jesus a second deity after God, another god deserving divine honors. Paul is, on the contrary, very sensitive to God's uniqueness. He does not hesitate to claim that God has acted through this man as he did through Abraham. If that last sentence had ended "as through Moses," the judgment of history might have been less severe on Paul. For good or ill, he thought the great lawgiver an interim figure, as he did the prophets and David. Adam the father of humanity and Abraham the father of believers were the great figures for Paul. They took their identity from Jesus Christ who, he was convinced, was a far greater one than either.

There is almost no limit to the intimacy with God that this Jesus now in glory possesses for Paul. His blood is "the means of expiation for all who believe,"[9] a reference to the annual sprinkling of blood on the bronze plate called the "mercy seat" in the holy of holies. God proves his love for us in that "while we were still sinners, Christ died for us."[10] This shedding of his blood will save us from God's wrath.[11] The "overflowing grace and gift of justice live and reign" in humanity through the one man Jesus Christ.[12] Christ, "once raised from the dead will never die again; death has no more power over him. His death was death to sin, once for all. His life is life to God."[13] Those God foreknew he predestined to "share the image of his son, that the son might be the firstborn of many brothers."[14] "If the spirit of him who raised Jesus from the dead dwells in you, then he who raised Christ from the dead will bring your mortal bodies to life also, through his spirit dwelling in you."[15]

---

9. Rom 3:25   10. Rom 5:8   11. See Rom 5:9   12. Rom 5:17
13. Rom 6:9–10   14. Rom 8:29   15. Rom 8:11

The list of Paul's appreciations of Jesus in conjunction with God could continue. Always he is "Christ" or "Lord" but always, too, a man in glory through whom God does something. God does it in sinful humanity ("flesh" for Paul), through his, God's, "spirit," which is none other than the spirit of Christ.

We have not yet referred to Paul's theory of the way Mosaic law is fulfilled in Christ and is no longer binding in its individual precepts. It certainly is not binding for gentiles.

In another, different sense it is not binding for Jews in terms of the details of rabbinic interpretation. This conviction has resulted in Paul's being considered in Jewish circles ever since a turncoat and a false Jew. We simply note this fact, turning our attention to who Paul thinks Jesus is that he can describe him as the "end (i.e., the fulfillment) of the law."

To approach Paul without emphasizing what some consider to be his much featured "anti-law" stance in Galatians and Romans may seem like playing Hamlet without the Prince of Denmark. His conviction that faith in Jesus Christ is essential for salvation and, in effect, a rendering of the individual prescriptions of the law no longer binding is central to his gospel. This generalized conclusion resulted from Paul's personal experience in a number of Greek cities over a twenty-five year period, starting with his experience of the risen Christ. The conviction would doubtless not have been held so firmly were it not for claims unacceptable to Paul that the law was binding on gentiles and that faith in Christ was insufficient.

Like anyone rebuffed, Paul tried to make sense out of his experience. He arrived at some conclusions that were valid for him. He was, after all, trying an entirely new thing, namely, expanding the notions of gentile "proselyte" and "God-fearer," which he knew from his youth, to encompass a new situation. The situation was so novel that he devised a theory of Jewish-gentile relations such as no previous Jewish proselytizer had adopted. It was the exact opposite of what he might have proposed as a Pharisaic Jew. His faith in Christ risen made all the difference. It became the faith of the preponderantly gentile church.

An example may help. Some Israeli statesmen, perhaps now living, may take up the challenge of trying to achieve full political rights for every resident of that country. In principle it is a secular state, having no religious tests for office. In principle, too, it is ethnic. That is to say, the constitution does not contemplate that its prime minister will be an Arab, an Armenian, or a naturalized gentile Frenchman. Some future Israelis may conclude that their country is not a democracy in the full sense until such a possibility exists for all who hold Israeli citizenship. They should expect to be told that the proposal is without merit because it challenges the very principle on which the nation came into being.

Similarly, Paul worked out in principle an "Israel" which, as his contemporaries were quick to remind him, destroyed the very basis of the concept Israel (the Jewish people), one which was both racial and religious by definition. More accurately, he proposed a means of entry into the people Israel as he conceived it that did not require circumcision or the fidelity to the whole law that followed therefrom. That means of entry was the faith of Abraham, whether held by Jew or gentile. A predictable result followed. In Paul's "Israel" the gentiles who were the camel's nose under the tent became in a short time a Christian church with no room for the circumcised. Practically speaking, his praise for the Jews as his brothers and sisters, his kinsfolk the Israelites, became no more than the dimly remembered speech of Christian origins. Theirs, Paul wrote, are

> the adoption, the glory, the covenants, the law-giving, the worship, and the promises; theirs the patriarchs, and from them comes the messiah (I speak of his human origins).[16]

By the year 135 the Jewish people were simply not present in the Christian community in any great numbers. Paul's non-kinsfolk, the gentiles, did not experience any pressure from numbers of Jews in their midst to develop his *ad hoc* theology of Israel any further. There was nothing like the same pressure of numbers that had brought about his theological theorizing in the first place.

Paul could write of all humanity, Jewish and gentile:

> God is faithful, and it is he who called you to fellowship with Jesus Christ our Lord.[17]

---

16. Rom 9:3–5   17. 1 Cor 1:9

No one can lay a foundation other than the one that has been laid, namely, Jesus Christ.[18]

Do you not see that your bodies are members of Christ?[19]

If our hopes in Christ are limited to this life only, we are the most pitiable of men.[20]

God is the one who firmly establishes us along with you in Christ.[21]

He was acutely aware of the contrast between the present situation and the one he hoped for. It mirrored the discrepancy between the actual lot of Jesus in life and what was his by right:

While we live we are constantly being delivered to death for Jesus' sake, so that the life of Jesus may be revealed in our mortal flesh.[22]

You are well acquainted with the favor shown you by our Lord Jesus Christ; how for your sake he made himself poor though he was rich, so that you might become rich by his poverty.[23]

Paul was fully Jewish in spirit in every matter but one. He introduced a human intermediary with God because he thought he had to. This Jesus was a person such as Adam or Abraham or Moses had never been:

We demolish sophistries and every proud pretension that raises itself against the knowledge of God; we likewise bring every thought into captivity to make it obedient to Christ.[24]

Those who belong to Christ Jesus have crucified their flesh with its passions and desires. Since we live in the spirit let us follow the spirit's lead.[25]

The "flesh" did not mean sex to Paul. It was all that had gone before in the human story since Adam's sin. "Spirit" was all

18. 1 Cor 3:11   19. 1 Cor 6:15   20. 1 Cor 15:19   21. 2 Cor 1:21
22. 2 Cor 4:11   23. 2 Cor 8:9   24. 2 Cor 10:5   25. Gal 5:24–25

that now was in Christ, or ever would be. This was Jewish eon-thought, in itself familiar enough, but thoroughly modified by events. Two things were unfamiliar: the claim of a man risen from the dead; and his lordship of the cosmos that relativized covenant, circumcision, and law.

23

The
Son of God

ACCORDING TO THE GOSPELS, JESUS WAS SINGLEMINDEDLY
bent on doing the will of God. His great absorption was hastening
the reign of his Father. He seemed to have no difficulty in acknowledging that he himself had a central place in announcing this rule of
God, even of helping to bring it on. Yet there is nothing of what we
can be sure he said that indicated he was at ease with receiving the
honor due to God, whether from the crowds or from his disciples.
The notion was unthinkable in a Jewish context. The gospels record
the normal enthusiasm that attends the life of anyone God is working wonders through. They tell of a man united totally with God
absorbed in mystical prayer. All the titles visited on Jesus, culminating in the expression of faith of the doubting Thomas as he
viewed the wounds of the risen Jesus, "My Lord and my God!" are
the fruit of decades of reflection. These faith convictions that came
afterward were triggered by the claim of those who experienced
him risen from the dead.

There are a number of ways to grapple with the problem of what is called "the divinity of Christ." One is to say, with India and the Far East, that all humanity is divine in the measure that it overcomes the body and its demands. In this sense, the reported resurrection of Jesus is simply the manifestation of Brahman or his Buddha-nature. He could easily be for Asia a man who was made perfect in a short space. Judaism and Islam attack the problem differently. Since in those traditions no human can be divine in any sense, the claim that Jesus was divine is by definition a false one.

This leaves Christianity taking a middle position. For it, humanity is not God, although it is open to divinization in a broad sense in something called the order of grace. This transforming union with the divine is the legacy of every human being, or can be. In one case only, Christianity teaches, a man was so intimately united with deity that a unique claim can be made for him.

The man is Jesus.

The claim is that he is uniquely divine.

This means not only that all that can be said of any human can be said of Jesus, but also that all that can be said of God can be said of him.

What can be said of a human creature? Much, indeed, yet the mystery of human nature eludes us.

What can be said of God? Practically nothing. Chiefly that God is all that humanity is not, except for intelligence and love and will in an infinitely different order.

One mistake that Christians made from the start, like Jews and Muslims and everyone else, was to assume they knew what God was like. They then made a mistake quite their own by saying, as a matter of popular religion, that Jesus Christ was God walking the earth in the body of a man. These Christians who knew what God was like had no trouble in imagining how God would act as he walked the earth inside Jesus. "Because he was God," Jesus knew everything, could do everything, and endured everything until the brief earthly interlude was over.

When Christians say "Jesus is God," many are thinking thoughts like these. As it happens, the Christian church never taught this ghost-in-a-machine doctrine as its faith in Jesus Christ. It described this view on many occasions as heretical or false. This has not kept Christians from adhering to it in large numbers, even to this day. The Jew, the Muslim, and the official teaching of the church quite rightly think the mentality to be a false one. An important difference is that, while the first two call it absurd, the latter tolerates it in practice, largely because it cannot expunge it. Official teaching cannot successfully bring it into line with orthodoxy. The terms of popular religion escape the control of any normative action.

In the Christian case there are just enough statements in the New Testament to give rise to this false reading of who Jesus Christ is. The authors of the literature, being Jews or gentiles in the Jewish tradition, have got the question of Jesus Christ straight. They know he is a Jewish man with all the limitations and powers that go with being human, all the suffering and summons to greatness that go with being Jewish. Yet, faced with the mystery of the intimacy of this man with God, they struggle to express a human confrontation with the divine in him, which they are convinced has never happened in the world's history. This has to be a faith judgment; it cannot be a historical judgment. History can know and record something of Jesus, but it cannot believe in him.

We have already explored a pattern that Christians gravitated toward early, first, that of a divine wisdom that both was *of* God (and hence not God) yet was what God was. Here is what the author of the fourth gospel made of that divine, creative word or wisdom:

In the beginning was the word;
the word was in God's presence,
and what the word was, God was.
He was present to God in the beginning. . . .
The word became flesh
and made his dwelling among us,
and we have seen his glory. . . .[1]

The same hand inspired the words of the following epistle.

This is what we proclaim to you:
what was from the beginning,
what we have heard,

---

1. Jn 1:1-2, 14

what we have seen with our eyes,
what we have looked upon
and our hands have touched—
we speak of the word of life.
This life became visible;
we have seen and bear witness to it,
and we proclaim to you the everlasting life
that was present to the Father
and became visible to us.[2]

Not only was this life visible but "our hands have touched it," a groping with words to express the conviction that the invisible God has been experienced in the person of the man Jesus.

The figure of speech "word" does not emerge as dominant, however, in early Christian writing. It occurs only at the beginning of John's gospel, in the first epistle of John, and once in the book of Revelation.[3] Jesus' use of the title "Father" for God seems to have made the figure of speech "son" the prevailing one for him in the earliest Christian books. It is figurative because properly a son is the male offspring of human parents. Any relation between a human being and the creator God that is described in the language of human begetting is metaphorical. This is a special case of the broader situation that all human language about God is metaphor.

The author of the first epistle of John writes:

Anyone who denies the son
has no claim on the Father,
but he who acknowledges the Father
can claim the son as well.[4]

This kind of writing has become standard within six or seven decades of Jesus' lifetime. A relation to Jesus is declared necessary if anyone is to have a relation with God. Matthew has Jesus say:

Everything has been given over to me by my Father. No one knows the son but the Father and no one knows the Father but the son—and anyone to whom the son wishes to reveal him.[5]

---

2. 1 Jn 1:1–2   3. See Rv 19:13   4. 1 Jn 2:23   5. Mt 11:27

The theme is pervasive in the fourth gospel:

Father, the hour has come!
Give glory to your son
that your son may give glory to you,
inasmuch as you have given him authority
     over all mankind,
that he may bestow everlasting life on
     those you have given him.
Everlasting life is this:
to know you, the only true God,
and him whom you have sent, Jesus Christ.[6]

It is clear that any human son of God who is as essential to man's knowledge of God and his enduring happiness as Jesus is must be very close to God indeed. John alone, among the four who wrote gospels, situates this son of man with God before "he came down from heaven."[7] Matthew and Luke do something similar in their accounts of Jesus' birth of a virgin by the power of God's spirit. The same tendency is found in certain fragments of hymns scattered through writings of the Pauline school. For example:

He was manifested in the flesh,
     vindicated in the spirit;
Seen by the angels,
     preached among the gentiles,
Believed in throughout the world,
     taken up to glory.[8]

The introduction leading into this lyrical outburst, which surely must have had a lively career in song when Christians gathered, was: "Wonderful, indeed, is the mystery of our faith, as we say in professing it. . . ."[9] Another, similar, song of praise runs like this:

Though he was in the form of God,
     he did not deem equality with God
     something to be grasped at.

---

6. Jn 17:1-3   7. Jn 3:13   8. 1 Tm 3:16bcd   9. 1 Tm 3:16a

Rather, he emptied himself
    and took the form of a slave,
    being born in the likeness of men.[10]

Heracles, the son of Zeus and the model ruler of Stoic political doctrine, was called "equal to God." In later times, so were the
Roman emperors. Plutarch points out in his life of Alexander the
Great that that sovereign did not overrun Asia for purposes of
plunder but to spread the gospel of Hellas over the barbarian
world. Jesus in the same way did not snatch selfishly the title of
"equal to God" but chose the lowliness of human estate, even
death, to achieve a great good for others.

This use of pagan models to convey the reality of Jesus to a
Greek world understandably makes Jewish thinkers nervous. It
provides them at the same time with a certain comfort. They sense
a development toward the deification of Jesus that is impossible to
Judaism. The comfort is diminished somewhat when passages in
praise of Jesus are examined that show an affinity to the cosmic
thought of Jewish writings of the apocalyptic and rabbinic periods.
Thus, the following from the Epistle to the Colossians betrays
distinct traces of thought which, while Stoic-influenced, are close
to certain Jewish speculations:

He is the image of the invisible God, the first-born of all
creatures. In him everything in heaven and on earth was
created, things visible and invisible, whether thrones or domi-
nations, principalities or powers, all were created through
him, and for him. He is before all else that is. In him, everything continues in being. It is he who is head of the body, the
church; he who is the beginning, the first-born of the dead, so
that primacy may be his in everything. It pleased God to
make absolute fullness reside in him and by means of him, to
reconcile everything in his person, both on earth and in the
heavens, making peace through the blood of his cross.[11]

That kind of thing was being written by Jewish thinkers
about an Adam who was framed large in the cosmos, or a Second
Man who at the end would fulfill the promise of the First Man. The

---

10. Phil 2:6-7   11. Col 1:15-20

Jew may not be pleased by certain Moses, Elijah, and son-of-man legends from the Jewish past that closely resemble the gospel portrait of Jesus, just as the Christian is not pleased to learn that the Alexander legend or the rhetoric of emperor worship contributed to later New Testament vocabulary about Christ. Both might say impatiently, betraying an ignorance of their own traditions, "But we have no such mythology as that!"

We all have such a mythology, if we are in any religious tradition at all. Far from being something to be ashamed of, it is proof of our centuries-old struggle to express something of the unspeakable God. How else can he be known except through tales, through poetry, through laws, through historical persons? And what is religious myth if not an amalgam of all these with the Ineffable lying behind it all?

Early believers in Jesus Christ thought that they knew God through a historical person. To them, he outran history, spanned the ages, had a prehistory in the bosom of God.

You cannot utter a word about God unless you do it by way of creatures. One way to speak of him is to deny that God is anything like creatures. Another is to say that he is like human creatures under certain aspects, with all their limitations removed. Still another is to speak of God as possessing in eminent degree all the perfections, whether actual or possible, of all creatures. The earliest Christians, faced with the eminent holiness of the risen Christ, began to say that to know this man was to know as much as could be known of God.

God's word dwelt in him.

God's spirit vivified him.

In the finite frame of his manhood he could not, of course, "take in" the absolute fullness of God; no human being can do that. Hence, the man Jesus thinking the thoughts of God with the aid of brain and central nervous system is a contradiction in terms. Whatever the "divinity of Christ" means, it cannot mean that. But all that the phrase can mean, the New Testament writers affirmed in a variety of ways, it does mean.

There was a man, they said, to whom the infinite God was more intensely present than to any other. This person has a purpose in the plan of God for all humanity, his fellow creatures, such as no one has. All things exist for him in that he is somehow central to the human story. This man and God are in an intimate conjunction that is basically inconceivable to us, but no less real for that. To know him is to know God in him.

This true man is "true God"—a phrase of the fourth-century creed of Nicaea—because the Father has begotten him from his own being as his only son. An eternal word was spoken to him in time, a word of God that is no less than God himself. In language such as this, the bishops at the Council of Nicaea spelled out what the scriptures said to them about Jesus Christ.

How much of what the early councils taught was part of Jesus' human awareness? How much of the mystery of the divine being did he know in his human being? All of that is hidden from the human eye, the Christian's eye of faith as much as anyone else's. The Christian can only say, "Jesus knew about God what it is possible for a man to know about God." The Christian goes on to say of the word spoken in Christ: What God was, he was.

Is the whole thing perhaps a yearning, a striving of the human heart that has decided to put the full weight of godhead on the frail shoulders of the pious Jew Jesus?

Only religious faith in him, or the absence of it, can answer that question.

The fact is that from the time some witnesses first experienced Jesus as risen, they knew they had a problem about God and humanity that none of their people had ever had before. They solved it by declaring their faith in God in this man, this man as a unique incarnation of the living God.

24

The
Three Who
Are God

John Donne is remembered for a sonnet that takes its title from the first line,

Batter my heart, three-personed God; for you
As yet but knock, breathe, shine, and seeke to mend.

He ends by asking to be imprisoned, enthralled, and ravished, but not before declaring that he labors to admit the God he has addressed, until now, to no purpose:

Reason your viceroy in mee, mee should defend,
But is captiv'd and proves weake or untrue,

It is not entirely clear who "your enemy" is, to whom the poet finds himself betrothed "like an usurped town to another due." We conclude that he is committed to what makes him unchaste and in that sense unfree.

The churchman struggling with his passions was no new figure in the seventeenth century. What may surprise us about Donne in the twentieth is that while reason is regrettably weak against "your enemy," this viceroy is cheerfully enlisted in supplicating a "three-personed God." Many will think the poet's struggle with the flesh inconsequential by contrast to the resident demon of the assumption of a holy trinity.

For if there is one betrayal of the spirit of Jesus that is most deeply resented, it is the church's "promotion" of him to membership in the trinity of Father, Son, and Holy Spirit. To many, that seems an unconscionable tampering with the notion of God. To others, especially in our day, it is an even more offensive tampering wih the human person of Jesus.

"Person" is the operative word here. It became such in the debates of the fourth century. It has caused much of the mischief since. "Person" is a correct word in modern speech for an individual human being. If you apply it to angels or devils or God you are altering its sense. You do less altering in those cases than if you use "person" of an animal or a river or the sun, but you are changing the meaning of the word nonetheless. We are back to the problem of analogy raised in the last chapter: using human words like "father," "word," and "wisdom" with respect to God. Humanity, having no language other than its own, is in trouble from the start in describing a deity that is quite unlike it.

Three persons means three people to most ears. When the word is applied to godhead it sounds like three gods. The followers of Jesus at the start were firmly Jewish. The least hint of a plurality of gods would have been as repulsive to them as to any Jew. It is commonly supposed outside Christian circles that when the church branched out toward the gentile world of paganism it acquired a "soft policy" on plurality in deity. It is heard compromising the stern monotheism of the Jew by admitting not a second god or consort but, worse still, a creature as a second like to God.

After three centuries of the existence of Christianity in a Greek-dominated world, an Alexandrian presbyter named Arius tried to solve, head on, the problem of who exactly Jesus was. He said of the word or son who was known, in time, as Jesus that there was "a [time] when he was not." The word of God for Arius was the first-born of all creatures, the one through whom everything else was made. The council held at Nicaea near Constantinople in 325 rejected Arius's well-intended suggestion. It wished to protect the divine in Jesus and not settle for this *logos* in him as the summit of creaturehood.

How did Christianity get into this complicated verbal situation? Why did it hammer out creeds, using philosophical language to do so, when it had a collection of its own inspired writings coupled with the Hebrew Bible to guide it? We mentioned earlier that Paul is usually blamed for "making Jesus God" on some pagan-religion principle. But that is not a very accurate insight into the problem. Paul is, if anything, clearer than other New Testament writers using the word "God" for God and always distinguishing God from Jesus. It is true, he calls Jesus "the Lord" consistently. In a Greek sense, this word could connote divine status well beyond the Aramaic *mar* that underlay the first level of the gospels—"lord" or "master." Paul and his followers freely described Jesus as close to God in unheard-of ways, as Chapter 22 pointed out. But Paul is an unlikely figure as the singlehanded culprit in deifying Jesus. The responsibility must be distributed among all who had a hand in framing the books of the New Testament.

Matthew provides a baptismal formula toward the end of his gospel (written about the year 85) containing three names or titles in conjunction with a single activity of God. This formula is presumed to be the one in use in Matthew's Syrian church. In it, Jesus speaks of himself as someone full authority has been given to in heaven and on earth:

> Go, therefore, and make disciples of all the nations.
> Baptize them in the name
>   of the Father,
>   and of the son,
>   and of the holy spirit.
> Teach them to carry out everything I have commanded you.
> And know that I am with you always, until the end of
>   the age.[1]

---

1. Mt 28:18–20

Most Bibles capitalize "Son" and "Holy Spirit," even though there are no capital letters anywhere in the earliest copies of the gospels. Two besides God under the title Father seem to be associated with God in this rite of initiation. They seem, moreover, to be both personal and on the level of godhead. The same problems would arise, of course, if there were a formula of dedication of individuals "in the name of God and the holy archangels Michael and Raphael." But immediately it can be stated that no claim was made by Christians that angelic beings were on a par with God, despite a few puzzling phrases in that vein in early writings.

Jesus of Nazareth is a person in the ordinary sense of the word, not the transferred sense. Since the other two, Father and Spirit, are not, we need to ask who is being designated "the son" for baptismal purposes. Is it Jesus, the man of Nazareth who is now in glory as the Christ? Is it someone who was God's son before he became Jesus of Nazareth? God does not have a son or sons in the human sense. He is not a father in the ordinary sense of either the whole human race or of one person in particular. If, however, the seeming balance of the three means that the evangelist thinks of them as equal in the work of making people Christians, we have in Jesus a "son" in an accommodated sense. The impossibility of finding adequate human language to speak about God is evident. The question remains, nonetheless: What did Matthew mean by baptizing Christians in those names, one of which unmistakably stands for God?

The word we translate as "person" (actually "subsistence" comes closer to the Greek) does not appear in the New Testament. It was borrowed much later from philosophy, not to muddy the waters but to make them clearer. A large question is: Has it had this effect? Better put: Did it clarify things at one time but fail to do so increasingly since that time? What word usage in the writings of the earliest Christians inclined later Christians to seize on "person" as the best term to convey the relation of these three to humanity and to each other?

The New Testament, like the Hebrew Bible, conceives of God personally. The limitations of creaturehood removed from him, he is someone who "thinks" and "wills" in an infinite, suprahuman way. He is intelligent and free; he is a responsible center of activity, not a life force. The New Testament writers did nothing to disturb this Jewish set of language assumptions regarding the God they called Father. They had a story to tell about his activity on the earth. They engaged in no new speculations on what he was like in heaven beyond the fact that the wisdom "at his side," or the word that he "spoke," had the Jesus of their concern as its human subject. That word dwelt in him. That wisdom was shown forth in him. "And what God was, the word was."

The New Testament writers believed that God eternally possessed wisdom or a word or, as the Jews lacking the Greek concept of eternity would say, "from everlasting." The "son" Jesus preexisted the world in the divine design; but then everything preexisted the world in the divine design. The difference for early Christians was, he did so in a special way. When, in time, the man Jesus was to be conceived and born, it would happen by God's everlasting power (or "holy spirit," to use Luke's term).[2] In him the word would become flesh and take up his dwelling among us.[3]

Except for a few hints at philosophical vocabulary to describe the providential plan, the New Testament writers cared only for what God had done for humanity in time. What he was like in himself did not engage them. An important difference was that, when the church became Greek in its throught patterns and vocabulary, the question of what God was like within himself began to engage it very much.

Jesus' death and resurrection as the means for humanity to lay hold of the reign of God, or salvation, or righteousness, or life, was the chief thing God had done for it. The New Testament insistence on God's presence in Jesus, as the latter went about doing the Father's will, can only derive from the impact Jesus made. From the days of his risenness onward, he lived in human memory as more than a prophet and as different from another god. In brief, he was something new in human history, a man totally indwelt by God. To use biblical language, he was indwelt by the word and the spirit of God. "God, in Christ, was reconciling the world to himself. . . ,"[4] is the way Paul expressed this indwelling action. "In Christ the fullness of deity resides in bodily form,"[5] is another mode of expression. "My God will supply your needs fully, in a

---

2. See Lk 1:35   3. See Jn 1:14   4. 2 Cor 5:19   5. Col 2:9

way worthy of his magnificent riches in Christ Jesus,"[6] Paul writes
his Macedonian converts. Jesus came to be thought of as an equal
to God, or in some sense God, partly because of phrases like these
from the pens of Paul and his disciples. God was in him as he was in
no other.

There is more to this, of course, chiefly the constant association of "God" and "Christ" in Paul's letters. Most especially there is
the easy substitution of the one for the other in descriptions of what
God had done for people who believe. It is as if God had been accessible before through covenant and law, but was even more so
now. In Christ there is recent, tangible proof of God with us. This
idea came tumbling out onto paper in dozens of Paul's phrases:

> All glory to our God and Father for unending ages! Amen.
> Give my greetings in Christ Jesus to every member of the
> church. . . . May the grace of the Lord Jesus Christ be with
> you.[7]

> You took me to yourselves as an angel [messenger] of God,
> even as if I had been Christ Jesus![8]

> Each one of you is an offspring of God because of your faith
> in Christ Jesus![9]

> To the God who alone is wise, may glory be given through
> Christ Jesus for endless ages.[10]

> Thanks be to God who has given us the victory through our
> Lord Jesus Christ.[11]

This association of the two in the one work is a constant in
Paul's epistles. Distinct as they are, God is not seen as accomplish-
ing the work of human sanctification without the other, Christ.
Those who save are two, God and Jesus Christ. The deed is one.

Another form of this twofold pattern of speech is found consistently in the last book of the New Testament, which is entitled
"the Revelation God gave to Jesus Christ."[12] In one of the visions
recorded there, members of a huge crowd cry out in a loud voice:

---

6. Phil 4:19   7. Phil 4:20-21, 23   8. Gal 4:14   9. Gal 3:26
10. Rom 16:27   11. 1 Cor 15:57   12. Rv 1:1

"Salvation is from our God, who is seated on the throne, and from the Lamb."[13] Again, this book says in a poem of praise:

Now have salvation and power come,
the reign of our God and the authority of his Anointed.[14]

This language does not put God and creature on a par so much as it praises the work of the one God through his human agent, figuratively described as a slaughtered Passover lamb and an anointed king. Jesus Christ is here quite indistinguishable from God under the aspect of the work done for humanity.

The holy spirit of God, or simply his spirit, is a Hebrew way of describing God's action in the world. Breath, like blood, was life for the ancient Semite; wind was power from a source unseen. It is no wonder, then, that wind or breath is a longstanding biblical way of speaking about God. Luke is most given of all the New Testament writers to describing God's action in Christ under this biblical figure, but he is not alone. The conception and birth of the child Jesus is for him a work of God's spirit. John the Baptizer tells the crowd that Jesus will baptize in holy spirit and fire. This same spirit descends on Jesus at his baptism, fills him upon his return from the Jordan, and leads him out into the desert to fast. Jesus returns in the power of the spirit to Galilee. Luke does not return to the theme of the spirit in so many words in the rest of his gospel, but in his book of Acts nothing happens in the early Jerusalem community without the spirit's prompting. John does something similar in reporting Jesus' promise of another paraclete or advocate, a divine agent who will recall to the disciples in Jesus' absence all that he did and taught while among them.

At a church council at Chalcedon (in modern Turkey) in 451, more than a century and a quarter of theological struggle came to an end in a verbal compromise. Needless to say, it did not heal the scars that had led up to it. The contesting parties were the followers of Eutyches, who stressed what was God in Christ, and the followers of Nestorius who protected what was man in Christ. Both parties professed the faith of Nicaea (325) that he was God and man but they professed it differently from each other; and one

---

13. Rv 7:10   14. Rv 12:10

of them differently from Nicaea, as a council at Ephesus (431) had declared against Nestorius. The formula of Chalcedon attempted compromise. It said that in Christ there were two natures, the nature of God and the nature of man, the two existing simultaneously "without commingling, without change of either, individually, and inseparably" in this "one and the same Christ who is the only Son and Lord." These natures are found in the "one person and one subsistence," not in "two persons [of Christ], distinct and separate."

An important thing happened in the next fifty years. It was popularly assumed that that person was a divine person, an eternal son, two ideas Chalcedon had had nothing to say about. This popular orthodoxy carried the day against the guarded teaching of the council itself. The Second Council of Constantinople (553) made this view specific—namely, that the one person in Jesus is divine—by condemning the opposite opinion. The full human status of Jesus, God's "son" in the New Testament, has been maintained with difficulty ever since by this making the "one person" of Chalcedon a divine person, something it did not say and the New Testament does not say. The closest the New Testament comes to Chalcedon is in portraying a man who is fully divine.

The only difference among the three persons, as St. Augustine of Hippo (d. 430) taught the mystery, was in individuation. This arose from the Father's eternal non-origination, and the Son's and the Spirit's eternally coming forth from the Father. In brief, the mystery of God's action in time became for the church the mystery of God's inner being in eternity. The Greek Christians and their Latin counterparts had to know how things were with God. Not surprisingly, they came to know.

God is so far beyond us, so deep within us that to say he is "three persons" in the sense intended cannot do violence to whatever he may be. There can be no question of a literally numerical three, any more than that God is a male. "Person" cannot apply strictly to God or the Spirit as it does to the one indisputable person in the affair, Jesus, because of the limits of all divine-human analogy. This means that the "three persons in one God" is a Greek way of expressing the New Testament truth—with a definiteness and assurance the New Testament may invite but does not employ—that God saves humanity through the "son" Jesus, and that ever since Jesus' glorification God breathes life into a dead world through the "spirit."

The God who does this, say the Christian creeds, must resemble what he does. That is all they say because it is all they can say. Our race can know no more of God than what it learns from seeing God operate in its midst.

The Christian church has much work undone that lies ahead. It must expound the mystery of Jesus Christ and the Holy Spirit in a way comprehensible to the Jew and the Muslim, neither of whom thinks like a Greek or a Roman.

It must do the same for the persons of India, of China, of Japan, of Black Africa.

It is a task well worth doing if Jesus is the man the gospels show us and if the Spirit of God is experienced at work in the world.

In doing this, the Christian church may also expound the mystery of Jesus Christ and the Holy Spirit to the satisfaction of its own members, fifteen centuries after Chalcedon. Which is the way the work is likely to begin.

25

The
Jesus of
the Qu'ran

JUDAISM AS A BODY DISREGARDED JESUS IN ITS WRITINGS because his followers, on the basis of knowing him, went in another direction than the followers of Hillel and Yoḥanan ben Zakkai. If the Galilean saint Jesus made an impression on the wider Jewish consciousness, it is not recorded. The only references to him in the Talmud are late in origin and unreliable. They cast doubts on the legitimacy of his birth (suggesting perhaps that Matthew's infancy story was available to them in some form) and they speak of his death at the Passover. In doing so, they provide certain details other than those of the gospels.

We have indicated the form that Christian teaching took in its insistence that God was in Christ through the word and in the world through the vivifying spirit. A threefold presence of God in history seemed to demand a threefold presence of God in heaven. This is an affirmable proposition once its terms are understood, if only because it bears so little relation to any this-worldly threeness.

A fairly extensive literature arose in the two hundred years after Jesus' death that goes by the name of the "apocryphal" or spurious gospels. These are works of piety and imagination that derive in spirit from the four gospels accepted by the church as normative for faith (hence "canonical"). The apocryphal literature is explicit, replete with the miraculous, and unmarked by reserve. Authorship by apostles is claimed in almost every case, in one case even by Jesus himself. Occasionally an apocryphal gospel will breathe a particular sectarian spirit. Some are gnostic in tone, meaning that they press the case for spirit over matter and propose salvation by way of a special knowledge (gnōsis) hidden from all but the elect.

We possess in brief quotation but not in their entirety a Nazarene Gospel and a Gospel of the Hebrews, both of which seem to have circulated among Christian Jews. These reportedly entertain a difficulty with the notion of Jesus' virgin birth. They feature acceptance of him as the deliverer of the Jewish people in the role of messiah. Needless to say, the specification of his eternal sonship of God in anything like Greek terms is missing from such documents. Writings like these, fragmentary as they are and reported by others (men like Hegesippus, Epiphanius, and Jerome), indicate what faith in Jesus might have been if acceptance of him had been confined to Jewish circles.

It is impossible, however, to reconstruct with perfect hindsight a Jewish Christianity. Traces of it remained alive in the Near East, chiefly Syria and Mesopotamia, for six or seven centuries after Jesus' lifetime. This tradition was fully Semitic but not Jewish. It bore the stamp of Osroene and the Euphrates valley. The Hellenistic features of the Christianity that developed out of Alexandria, Antioch, and Constantinople (Jerusalem was not a possibility, after its final destruction as a Jewish city by Hadrian in 138) were largely absent from this Eastern expression of faith in Jesus.

There were both Christian and Jewish communities of some vigor in southern Arabia in the seventh century when Islam came to the fore. Islamic faith did not derive directly from either tradition but was a purified version of the monotheism of some Arabian tribesmen. It struggled hard to dislodge from popular acceptance the preponderant idol-worship of those parts. Attempts had previously been made by both Jews and Christians to convert the native

Arabian population to their ways of belief. The Qur'an (the "Reading") bears the stamp of those efforts. For our purposes, the view of Jesus available to outsiders and reported on in the Qur'an is of interest. Important to note is the greater measure of detail from the apocryphal gospels than that deriving from the four canonical ones. This leads to speculation on the nature of the Arabian Christianity to which Muhammad and the first generation of his followers were exposed.

Sûrah XIX of the Qur'an, an early Meccan composition, is entitled in Arabic *Maryam* and has to do with Jesus' mother. It tells of the conception and birth of John son of Zechariah, much in the manner of the gospel account. The appearance of an angel to Mary is reported. She "whom no mortal has touched" will bear a faultless son, the angel tells her. Mary withdraws to a distant place and takes refuge in the trunk of a date-palm. Its fruit sustains her, as does a tiny stream that appears at her feet. When Mary brings her child to her own people—him whom the angel had called "a revelation for mankind and a mercy from Us"—she hears a defense of her chastity in what seems to be a refutation of slurs on Jesus' parentage: "Oh, sister of Aaron! Your father was not a wicked man nor your mother a harlot."[1] A verse in Sûrah XXIII, *The Believers*, will have Allah say in praise of mother and son: "And We made the son of Mary and his mother a portent, and We gave them a refuge on a height, a place of flocks and water-springs."[2]

Sûrah III, *The Family of 'Imran*, has Jesus speaking from his cradle in the manner of accounts of his precocious behavior found in the apocrypha.[3] From that infant setting, the child says in Surah XIX:

Behold! I am the slave of Allah. He has given
me the scripture and has appointed me a prophet.
He has made me blessed wherever I may be, and
has enjoined on me prayer and almsgiving so long
as I remain alive,

---

1. Sûrah XIX, *Mary*, 28; see Sûrah III, *The Family of 'Imran*, for another account of Jesus' conception and Mary's upbringing, derived from the apocryphal gospels   2. Sûrah XXIII, *The Believers*, 50
3. Sûrah III, *The Family of 'Imran*, 46

And has made me dutiful to her who bore me, and
has not made me arrogant, unblest.
Peace on me the day I was born, and the day I
die, and the day I shall be raised alive.[4]

This description of Jesus as the "slave of Allah" (*'Abd Allah*) and a
"prophet" follows the tradition of early preaching about him in the
church.[5] Allah can find no higher praise for the son of Mary than to
cite his bondage to him which, as with the Isaian *"ebhed YHWH"*
(servant of the LORD), means liberation from all earthly servitudes.
Sûrah XLIII, *Ornaments of Gold*, expresses it this way:

He is nothing but a slave on whom We bestowed favor, and
We made him a pattern for the children of Israel. . . . When
Jesus came with clear proofs [of the sovereignty of Allah], he
said: I have come to you with wisdom, and to make plain
some of the things about which you differ. So fulfill your
duty to Allah, and obey me. See! Allah is my Lord and your
Lord. So worship him. This is the right path.[6]

The Qur'an never departs from its pattern of praise for the
prophet Jesus. Thus, Sûrah IV, *Women*, says that he is born into
the lines "of Abraham and Ishmael, Isaac and Jacob and the tribes,
and Jesus and Job and Jonah."[7] Yet the scripture of Islam has no
kind word to say of any special sonship of Allah he may enjoy. The
Sûrah on *Mary* declares: "It does not befit Allah that he should take
to himself a son. Glory be to him! When he decrees a thing he says
to it only: Be! and it is."[8] A warning is uttered to the Christians in
Sûrah IV. They, along with the Jews, are in general treated with
respect in the Qur'an as "people of the Book," meaning that both
have scriptures of their own.

O people of the Book! Do not exaggerate in your religion or
utter anything concerning Allah but the truth. The Messiah,
Jesus son of Mary, was only a messenger of Allah, and Allah's
word which he conveyed to Mary, and a spirit from him. So

4. Sûrah XIX, *Mary*, 30-33   5. See Acts 3:23-26
6. Sûrah XLIII, *Ornaments of Gold*, 59-60, 62-64   7. Sûrah IV, *Women*, 163
8. Sûrah XIX, *Mary*, 35, 88-93

believe in Allah and his messengers and do not say "Three."
Cease! It is better for you that way. Allah is only one God. It
is far removed from his transcendent majesty that he should
have a son. His is all that is in the heavens and on the earth.
And Allah is sufficient as defender. The Messiah will never
scorn to be a slave to Allah, nor will the favored angels.[9]

In an exhortation to believers, namely, those who follow the
path of Al-Islam ("The Surrender"), there is found the charge
against the children of Israel that they broke their covenant. As a
result, says Allah,

We have cursed them and made hard their hearts. They
change words from their context and forget a part of that
about which they are admonished. You will not cease to
discover treachery from all but a few of them. [One needs to
read a history of the birth of Islam to interpret this.] But bear
with them and love them. Behold, Allah loves those who are
kindly.

The same passage from Sûrah V, The Table Spread, continues:

And with those who say, "See! We are Christians," We
[Allah] made a covenant, but they forgot a part of that about
which they were admonished. For that reason We have stirred
up enmity and hatred among them until the day of resurrection, when Allah will inform them of their deeds.

O people of the Book! Now has Our messenger [Muhammad]
come to you, expounding to you much of what you used to
hide in the Scripture, and forgiving much. Now a light from
Allah has come to you, and a plain Scripture by which Allah
guides whoever seeks his good pleasure in the direction of
paths of peace. He brings them out of darkness into light by
his decree, and guides them toward a straight path. They, indeed, have disbelieved who say: "Behold! Allah is the
Messiah, son of Mary." Say [to them]: "Who then can do
anything except Allah if he had willed to destroy the Messiah,

---

9. Sûrah IV, Women, 171–72

son of Mary, and his mother and everyone on earth? Allah's is the sovereign rule of the heavens and the earth and all that is in between them, and the pilgrimage is to him.

O people of the Book! Our messenger has come to you now after an interval when there were no messengers, lest you should say, "There did not come to us a messenger of cheer nor anyone to warn us."[10]

It should be noted in passing that Christianity never taught that "God is Jesus" [Allah is the Masiḥ], only that Jesus is God, in the sense described in the previous two chapters. Something similar must be said of the charge of covenant-breaking by the Jews. The accusation may be taken directly from the Hebrew Bible, but it is more likely to have echoed a Christian complaint that the Qur'an finds congenial. It may also be a Muslim demand for biblical literalism in opposition to the Talmudic accommodation to cultural change.

The powerlessness of the son of Mary against Allah underscores his creaturehood, something maintained by the New Testament at all points but evidently thought by the Qur'an to be contradictory to the claim of divine power for Jesus. Says Sûrah III, "The likeness of Jesus with Allah is the likeness of Adam. He created him of earth. . . ."[11]

Jesus' calling, in the view of the Qur'an, was to confirm what was written before him in the Rotah, "and to make lawful some of that which was forbidden to you."[12] He came to the Jews with a sign from their LORD; they should therefore fulfill their duty to Allah and obey Jesus. Jesus depended much on his disciples, who became Allah's helpers. He also brought good tidings of a messenger who was to come after him, namely, the Praised One (Aḥmad), Muhammad. Yet, though Jesus came to them with clear proofs, namely, of Allah's sovereignty and his mercy, his hearers dismissed him by saying, "This is mere magic." The upshot was that a party of the children of Israel believed in him and a party did not. Sûrah LXI speaks of the outcome: "Then We strengthened

10. Sûrah V, The Table Spread, 13–19   11. Sûrah III, The Family of 'Imran, 59
12. III, 50; see Sûrah LXI, The Ranks, 6

those who believed against their foe, and they became the uppermost."[13] *The Family of 'Imran* makes a similar choice between
Christians and Jews:

> Remember when Allah said: "O Jesus! Behold, I gather you
> up and cause you to ascend to me, and am cleansing you of
> those who disbelieve and am setting those who follow you
> above those who disbelieve until the day of resurrection.
> Then you will all return to me and I shall judge between you
> as to that over which you used to differ."[14]

The same Qur'anic author is disturbed that Jews and Christians are not in agreement. He suggests as a basis for coming
together that none but Allah be worshipped and that no partner be
ascribed to him, nor "any of us take others for lords besides
Allah."[15]

A major difference between Jews and Christians over the
way Abraham figures as the father of the life of faith is evidently
known to the writer of this Sûrah. Paul, it may be recalled, invited
the readers of his letters written to Galatia and Rome to go back in
time before the interim settlement achieved through Moses and the
law. Paul proposed going back to Abraham, the father of all believers, to whom the fatherhood of many nations had been promised through his seed. Paul identified this seed as Jesus. The Qur'an
argues somewhat as Paul does, but unlike him makes the gospel as
expendable as the law. Addressing itself to Jews and Christians,
Sûrah III calls for a leap from Abraham to Muhammad, not as Paul
did, from Abraham to Christ:

> O people of the Book! Why will you argue about Abraham
> when the Torah and the Gospel were not revealed till after
> him? Have you no sense? You argue about those things you
> have some knowledge of. Why do you argue concerning mat-
> ters you know nothing about? Allah knows. You do not.
> Abraham was not a Jew nor was he a Christian; he was an
> upright man who had surrendered (*muslimun*), and he was
> not an idolater. Those of mankind who have the best claim to
> Abraham are those who followed him, and this prophet

---

13. LXI, 14   14. Sûrah III, *The Family of 'Imran*, 55   15. III, 64

[Muhammad] and those who believe (with him); and Allah is the protecting friend of believers. . . . It is not possible for any human being to whom Allah has given the scripture and wisdom and the prophet's office that he should afterward say to mankind: Be slaves of me instead of Allah: [what he said was]: Be faithful servants of the LORD by virtue of your constant teaching of the scripture and your constant study of it.[16]

In that last verse Islam has faithfully reflected what Jesus said and strongly reprobated what he did not say. Overall, however, the Qur'an does what all the religious traditions have done, none with any large measure of success. It asks all religious parties, Jews and Christians in particular, to desert their stands and to surrender: in a word, to believe as the writers do.

In the course of being challenged, both Jew and Christian are prone to say of the challenger: "He misconstrues my revelation. He rejects the caricature he takes to be my faith. But so do I." All parties withdraw, satisfied with the impregnability of their positions.

But the problem of Jesus remains.

It is the problem of a man who made so deep an impression on those who knew him that he could not control for all time to come their view of him. Either that is true or he could and did control it, depending on what you believe about him and about divine providence. Others have suffered the same fate, notably the Buddha who was taken for the unique expression of Brahman. Muhammad, it is clear from every page in the Qur'an, did not invite anyone to think of him as anything but a prophet. He takes constant measures to see to it that, after his death, his followers would construe him as no more than a faithful prophet-teacher.

Jesus discouraged attention to his person by concentrating wholly on God. Of his active effort to keep anyone from associating him too closely with God in the work of proclaiming the reign of God, we have but one instance, in Mark's gospel: "Why do you call me good? No one is good but God alone."[17] Jesus made the impression on people that he made. In being raised from the dead, he made a special impression. Everything else about him followed from that upraising from the tomb.

---

16. III, 65–68, 79   17. Mk 10:17–18

Such is the story of all the living religions. One may deplore them or delight in them. One cannot plot their course for them.

Their adherents have but a single question to answer, a sole responsibility to fulfill: Have they been faithful to the spirit of him who, under God or by "enlightenment," they claim as their founder? Jesus would be happy with that question. One of his followers, Luke, put it this way: "When the son of man comes, do you think he will find faith upon the earth?"[18]

---

18. Lk 18:8

Conclusion

AT THE CLOSE OF A BOOK ABOUT JESUS IT MAY FAIRLY BE asked whether a book about Jesus is possible. The reader may think so but suspect that this is not the book, or may think that no writing about him makes any sense but the four gospels, or that no writing about him including the four gospels makes any sense.

The last-named group is in the minority by any reckoning.

Jesus is thought by millions to be an interesting person and an important one, by those who call themselves Christians the most important one.

Whether he is thought of as mystic, saint, or sage, as way to God, or the only son of God, or any of the above in combination, is for the church that calls him Lord and for the individual in concert with that church to say.

In saying anything at all about him a writer says too much or too little; possibly both at once.

The wisest thing any reader can do about Jesus is go to the New Testament in the conviction of one's own lack of insight and ask the spirit of God for help to see what is there. But doing this in isolation is a practice entirely without an ancient history. It has always been done in a community of believers, which is the very meaning of "church."

Basic Resources

Danby, Herbert. *The Mishnah* (translated from the Hebrew with introduction and brief explanatory notes). Oxford: Clarendon Press, 1933.

Davies, Stevan L. *The Gospel of Thomas and Christian Wisdom* (including the Cartlidge-Dugan translation of the text of Thomas). New York: Seabury, 1983.

Dawood, N.J. *The Koran.* New York: Penguin Books, 1964.

Finegan, Jack. *The Archeology of the New Testament: The Life of Jesus and the Beginning of the Early Church.* Princeton, N.J.: Princeton University Press, 1978.

Gaster, Theodor H. *The Dead Sea Scriptures in English Translation* (revised and enlarged edition). New York: Doubleday Anchor, 1964.

Grollenberg, Luc. *Shorter Atlas of the Bible.* New York: Nelson, 1959.

Herford, R. Travers (tr.). *Pirke Aboth. The Ethics of the Talmud: Sayings of the Fathers.* New York: Schocken Books, 1962.

Josephus, Flavius. *Antiquities of the Jews.* Cambridge, Mass.: Harvard University Press, 1969.

Schein, Bruce E. *Following the Way: The Setting of John's Gospel.* Minneapolis: Augsburg, 1980.

Vermes, Geza. *The Dead Sea Scrolls in English.* New York: Penguin, 1962.

———. *The Dead Sea Scrolls: Qumran in Perspective.* Philadelphia: Fortress Press, 1981.

Index

Citations

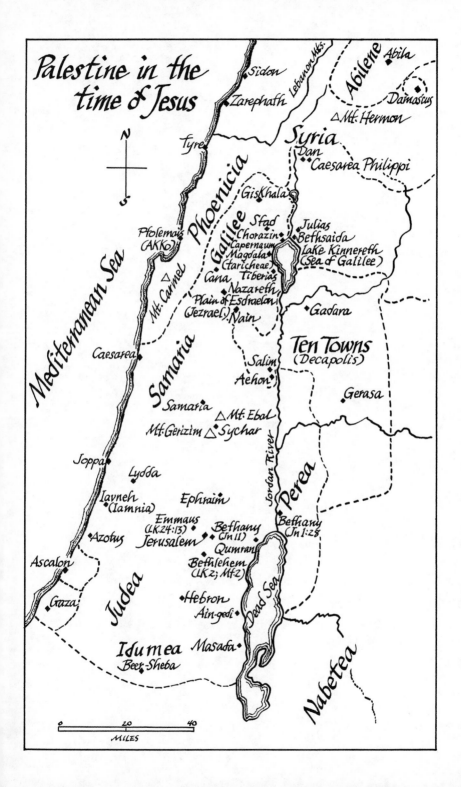

Palestine in the
time of Jesus

Mediterranean Sea

Sidon
Zarephath
Tyre
Phoenicia
Ptolemais (AKKO)
Mt. Carmel
Galilee
GisKhala
Sfad
Chorazin
Capernaum
Magdala (Taricheae)
Cana
Tiberias
Nazareth
Plain of Esdraelon (Jezrael)
Nain
Caesarea
Samaria
Samaria
Mt. Ebal
Mt. Gerizim
Sychar
Salim
Aehon
Joppa
Lydda
Ephraim
Iavneh (Iamnia)
Emmaus (LK 24:13)
Azotus
Jerusalem
Bethany (Jn 11)
Qumran
Ascalon
Bethlehem (LK 2; Mt 2)
Judea
Gaza
Hebron
Ain-gedi
Idumea
Masada
Beer-Sheba
Dead Sea

Syria
Abilene
Abila
Damascus
Mt. Hermon
Dan
Caesarea Philippi
Julias
Bethsaida
Lake Kinnereth (Sea of Galilee)
Gadara
Ten Towns (Decapolis)
Gerasa
Jordan River
Perea
Bethany (Jn 1:28)
Nabetea

N
S

0   20   40
MILES

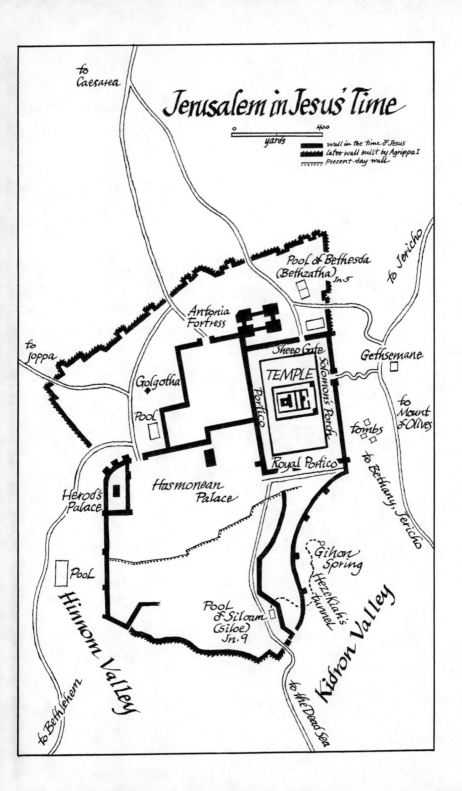

Jerusalem in Jesus' Time

0   400
yards

■■■ Wall in the time of Jesus
▬▬▬ later wall built by Agrippa I
▪▪▪ Present-day wall

to Caesarea

to Jericho

Pool of Bethesda (Bethzatha) Jn. 5

Antonia Fortress

to Joppa

Sheep Gate

Gethsemane

Golgotha

TEMPLE

Pool

Portico

Solomon's Porch

to Mount of Olives

tombs

Royal Portico

to Bethany, Jericho

Hasmonean Palace

Herod's Palace

Gihon Spring

Pool

Hezekiah's Tunnel

Pool of Siloam (Siloe) Jn. 9

Hinnom Valley

Kidron Valley

to Bethlehem

to the Dead Sea